We're each equipped with spiritual gifts to help us navigate adversity. *The Power of 3* is a simple yet powerful framework to create clarity on how you've been uniquely prepared to overcome the obstacles in your life.

JOHN BUTCHER, CEO of Caribou Coffee

Robb Hiller has crafted an amazing story of tenacity, courage, and survival. His harrowing life story is a vivid reminder that, even today, miracles do happen when you least expect them. Adversity never leaves us, he writes, which is so true. We all face our own personal trials and tribulations. God doesn't promise an easy life to any of us. It's how we cope with trials and adversity that define us—how we play the hand we're dealt. The eternal truths Robb discusses about asking, activating, and advocating can help anyone going through a rough patch, from family struggles to business challenges. The Power of 3 is real, and I predict that if you open your mind and your heart, this book can and will change your life.

PAUL DOUGLAS, WCCO radio show host, meteorologist, and serial entrepreneur

Robb has used a powerful and personal story to share a template for positive change—how to deal with life's inevitable setbacks and make the most of the life that God has given us. *The Power of 3* abounds with practical wisdom and encouragement on becoming a valued mentor, friend, or parent. Anyone in a position of leadership can benefit from this book.

JERRY MATTYS, former CEO of Tactile Medical

So much can be said about Robb Hiller's amazing book, *The Power of 3*. However, one simple but powerfully life-changing word filled my being over and over again: *hope*. We all need it. This book gives it.

TOM LEHMAN, PGA Tour golfer, winner of the British Open, and the only golfer in history to have been awarded the Player of the Year honor on all three PGA Tours

The three fundamental questions of life are *Who am I?*, *Why am I here?*, and *Where am I going?* Robb taps into the Power of 3 resources that bring clarity to these life-giving questions. Your mind will be stretched, your heart enlarged, and your passions ignited when you discover the Power of 3 and apply it to your everyday life and relationships.

DR. JOEL K. JOHNSON, lead pastor of Westwood Community Church

Robb Hiller has written a very helpful and practical guide to being a better leader and a better person. It brings together concepts that might be familiar to readers of Edgar Schein, Carol Dweck, or Chip Heath and translates them into practical approaches that can be immediately applied. I would recommend Robb's book to anyone who is committed to the improvement of their community, organization, family, or themselves.

JAMES HEREFORD, president and CEO of Fairview Health Services

Robb Hiller should not be here. Although a seemingly unsurvivable diagnosis should have claimed his life, he not only survived but thrived. In *The Power of 3*, Robb shares the process he's learned throughout the journey that freed him to embrace the possibility of his life. In reading *The Power of 3*, you'll be liberated to embrace the possibility in your life too.

JOHN O'LEARY, #1 national bestselling author of *On Fire* and *In Awe*

THE POWER OF 3

BEAT ADVERSITY
FIND AUTHENTIC PURPOSE
LIVE A BETTER LIFE

THE
POWER
OF
3

ROBB HILLER

The Tyndale nonfiction imprint

Visit Tyndale online at tyndale.com.

Visit Tyndale Momentum online at tyndalemomentum.com.

TYNDALE, Tyndale's quill logo, *Tyndale Momentum*, and the Tyndale Momentum logo are registered trademarks of Tyndale House Ministries. Tyndale Momentum is the nonfiction imprint of Tyndale House Publishers, Carol Stream, Illinois.

The Power of 3: Beat Adversity, Find Authentic Purpose, Live a Better Life

Cover photograph of multicolored hallway by Efe Kurnaz on Unsplash.com.

Author photograph taken by Rebecca Hahn Photography.

Interior photograph of bridge copyright © Ashish/Adobe Stock. All rights reserved.

Interior illustration of speaker icon copyright © bassile/Depositphotos. All rights reserved.

Interior illustration of amygdala copyright © VectorMine/iStockphoto. All rights reserved.

Designed by Ron C. Kaufmann with Alberto Navata

Edited by Jonathan Schindler

All Scripture quotations, unless otherwise indicated, are taken from the Holy Bible, *New International Version*,® *NIV*.® Copyright © 1973, 1978, 1984, 2011 by Biblica, Inc.® Used by permission. All rights reserved worldwide.

Scripture quotations marked NLT are taken from the *Holy Bible*, New Living Translation, copyright © 1996, 2004, 2015 by Tyndale House Foundation. Used by permission of Tyndale House Publishers, Carol Stream, Illinois 60188. All rights reserved.

For information about special discounts for bulk purchases, please contact Tyndale House Publishers at csresponse@tyndale.com, or call 1-800-323-9400.

Library of Congress Cataloging-in-Publication Data
Names: Hiller, Robb, author.
Title: The power of 3 : beat adversity, find authentic purpose, live a better life / Robb Hiller.
Other titles: The power of three Description: Carol Stream, Illinois : Tyndale House
    Publishers, [2020] | Includes bibliographical references.
Identifiers: LCCN 2020030946 (print) | LCCN 2020030947 (ebook)
    | ISBN 9781496447289 (hardcover) | ISBN 9781496447296 (kindle edition)
    | ISBN 9781496447302 (epub) | ISBN 9781496447319 (epub)
Subjects: LCSH: Self-actualization (Psychology) | Motivation (Psychology) | Goal
    (Psychology)
Classification: LCC BF637.S4 H5457 2020 (print) | LCC BF637.S4 (ebook)
    | DDC 158—dc23
LC record available at https://lccn.loc.gov/2020030946
LC ebook record available at https://lccn.loc.gov/2020030947

Printed in the United States of America

26	25	24	23	22	21	20
7	6	5	4	3	2	1

CONTENTS

CHAPTER 1

Hope Is Here: When Adversity Walks through the Door

Wherever there is no hope in the future, there is no power in the present.

JOHN MAXWELL

"ROBB!" A familiar voice called my name down a grocery store aisle. "I can't believe you're here!"

I smiled as Tommy excitedly waved both arms at me. "Well," I replied, "you can't believe how glad I am to be here. It's wonderful to see you."

For years, Tommy and I had been on-and-off basketball buddies. Now he grabbed me in a very public bear hug. When Tommy and I had last crossed paths six months prior, he'd concluded I didn't have long to live. "You were in tough shape then," he exclaimed. "You look so much better now!"

Our brief exchange reminded me how even our most casual relationships can be profound. Running into Tommy caused gratitude to well up inside me for the progress I had experienced in my battle against cancer, and I felt renewed joy at having a second chance to live.

As the founder and CEO of a nationally recognized consulting firm, I had long helped leaders and organizations across the country identify, attract, and develop talent. I am a certified professional behavior analyst, results coach, and talent-assessment expert who has evaluated more than twenty-three thousand individuals—everyone from business-to-business sales staff to senior leaders at Fortune 500 companies. I recently was recognized as one of the top consultants among several thousand of my colleagues and presented with the Bill Bonnstetter Lifetime Achievement Award.

But more than these accomplishments, the greatest validation of my work has been

the transformation I've seen as people have beaten adversity, found their true purpose, and broken through to a better life, at work and at home.

There was power behind my work. Over the years, I had discovered an astonishingly effective method for helping people get unstuck, conquer challenges, and dramatically change.

Yet when adversity struck close to home, that approach—indeed my whole outlook on how to succeed at work and life—was severely challenged.

Adversity Comes Home

Nine months before I ran into Tommy in that grocery store aisle, I awoke to a beautiful, sunny Thursday and was looking forward to exercising at my usual athletic club—a mix of working out inside and walking around the lake. The drive to the club made me smile. After long months of cold and snow, seeing green grass was *thrilling*. Golf season was almost here!

After a few minutes on the treadmill and a little weight lifting, I dropped to the ground and began performing planks, supporting myself on my elbows and holding my body in a rigid straight-backed pose. Almost immediately, pain jabbed my abdomen, like a hard punch in the stomach. Five minutes later, I tried again, with the same result.

What's going on? I thought.

I made an appointment with my doctor, and after checking me over the next day, he suspected a hernia and referred me for a CT scan. The day after that appointment I was in the tube for the scan and feeling nervous, anxious, and downright fearful. A few hours after my scan, I was swiveling in my desk chair at my home office, enjoying the view of the undeveloped wetland beyond our backyard, when my cell phone rang. It was my doctor. He didn't pause for niceties. "You have a large mass in your abdomen," he said. "It's definitely cancer, some type of lymphoma. We need you to come in for a biopsy."

I leaned back in my chair in shock. I'd known for three years that I had chronic lymphocytic leukemia. With the incurable cancer in its beginning stages, my doctors had chosen to keep an eye on it rather than treat it. Now I was hearing I had a second cancer.

I soon underwent tissue and bone marrow biopsies. The needle looked big enough to go completely through any part of my body. I had neck surgery to remove cancerous lymph nodes, which was followed by a PET scan.

Within a couple of weeks, I was in an oncologist's office, staring at colorful PET images of my insides. They showed a mass of bright red near my esophagus and stomach and throughout my insides.

I knew red wasn't good. The doctor's words went beyond my worst fears.

"You know you have leukemia," he said. "The scan shows you also have two other kinds of cancer." The new unwelcome invaders were diffuse large B-cell lymphoma, an aggressive form of non-Hodgkin lymphoma, and follicular lymphoma, another type of non-Hodgkin lymphoma.

"We'll begin treating the large B-cell right away, as this form is aggressive. We should be able to help you with that," the doctor went on. "As you know, there's no cure for the CL leukemia. And I'm sorry, but there's also no cure for the follicular lymphoma."

On top of the incurable cancer we had been

monitoring, I had not just one new cancer but two. "It looks like I got lucky," I said wryly. "I got the trifecta." Three deadly cancers were growing inside me.

As my wife, Pam, and I exchanged glances, tears filled our eyes. How was this even possible?

Your Challenges Large and Small

My experience happened to be acute, but life's circumstances come to us in all shapes and sizes. They put us on a journey we didn't choose, want, or expect.

Your own difficulties might be small-scale or far bigger than mine. They might come on suddenly or accumulate over time, one tough break after another. Whatever you face, you know how it feels to reach a point where you think, *This is really hard. I don't know if I can do it.*

- Maybe you have a lousy boss who sucks the joy out of your days. You can't help but wonder if you're on a short list to lose your job.
- Or you have family or friends who have grown distant. It wasn't that long ago that you felt

close, but now the calls and texts are rare. You're not sure what happened, but you feel alone.

• Perhaps you're struggling in your marriage. You've tried to convince your spouse to get counseling, but you're not sure yourself whether it will do any good.

• Or your kid is rebelling like a bull out of a barn. You're doing your best, but nothing works. You feel like you're losing your child.

• Maybe you're just getting started in your career. You've learned a lot in your studies, but you wonder how to move forward in real life. How do you pull everything together?

• Or you're in business, and sales are plummeting. Your team isn't getting it done, and nothing you try gets the results you need. You fear the company will dry up and blow away.

• Perhaps your faith is faltering. When you talk to God, the heavens feel like a cement ceiling. You're not happy with the state of your life, and you just don't know what to do.

Each of us could be struck by any of these problems and a million more. We begin to say, "This is bothering me. It has festered for a long time, and I still don't know how to address it. I don't have the strength to go on." We feel helpless—or at least really frustrated.

Setbacks are inevitable. We all experience them.

But I want to show you a method to help you move forward. It consists of easy-to-understand steps for life, which I discovered long ago and have successfully used with thousands of people in business and beyond, and it's the method I employed when faced with three deadly cancers. I call it the "Power of 3."

You can learn this method quickly—and put it into practice *immediately*. Through any adversity, the Power of 3 can transform your life, whether your frustrations are day-to-day annoyances or far more serious issues.

While I've coached people in these truths for many years, I felt a final nudge to put this message in book form when I spoke at my college reunion. After my talk, an old friend who led an esteemed orthopedic surgery practice said, "Robb, I can't tell you how much it meant to me to hear how you used the Power of 3 to make it through your cancer treatments. You need to share this with others."

Dr. Tom is known for his gruff, driven personality. Seeing him wipe away tears surprised me. "Thanks so much for your encouragement," I said. "Are those tears because my message was so bad?"

Dr. Tom laughed and reiterated that this message could help anyone. He planned to use it himself. His words were an unexpected confirmation to start writing.

I promised myself this wouldn't be just another business book, a few good tips wrapped in far too many words. Failure has been a great teacher to me over the years, and I have experienced it many times. But when I discovered the principles captured in the Power of 3, they guided and transformed my life. More important, they will make all the difference for you. This isn't a book to read and then put on a shelf.

It conveys practical wisdom and life-giving encouragement that I hope you'll come back to again and again.

Out of the Ditch

When I was in my forties, I was looking for a fresh start in my career. For years I had led a telecommunications company as the CEO, but one of my greatest passions was helping people, and I wanted to try consulting work. I worked with a friend for close to a year before launching my own consulting business, Performance SolutionsMN.

Initially, I focused on guiding companies in sales growth, leadership training, and strategic planning. I was also introduced to Target Training International, an Arizona-based organization that provided science-based personal-assessment tools. The more I delved into the world of assessments, the more I realized their potential for pinpointing trouble spots in company practices and relationships and for identifying potential solutions.

By combining these new tools with my own analysis, I began helping firms evaluate and hire candidates and place the right people in the right jobs. My clients observed dramatic improvements, which pleased them and excited me. They used words like *empowering* and *inspiring* to describe my impact. They were also thrilled with the upward growth in their profit margins.

As my consulting business grew and I worked with more clients, repeatable principles began to jump out to me as consistently effective.

For example, there was the fiery software company chairman who insisted his sales team was hiding low sales and poor performance behind complaints about the software itself. To calm him down, I asked a pair of simple questions: "In an ideal situation, how would you want your customers to respond to your software? What might they say that would indicate you're on track?"

Shifting the chairman's perspective from blaming his staff for poor sales to the goal of having satisfied customers quickly calmed him down. I began to see that asking the right questions could make a powerful difference in changing attitudes and eliciting vital information.

Another time, I was hired to help Eyal, the young director of operations for a medical device company, reorganize his department and cut costs. A survey of the staff also identified communication issues. Eyal was relatively inexperienced and younger than most of his team, so we faced a significant challenge. I soon discovered, however, that Eyal's talents more than made up for his inexperience.

With my encouragement, he used his natural optimism, genuine personality, and conflict-resolution skills to inspire the team to catch his vision for the department. Eyal also shifted the responsibilities of his staff to better utilize their abilities. The outcome was a much more cohesive and effective team, as well as cost savings that reached $1 million within a year. Those impressive improvements were the result of Eyal activating his natural gifts, then putting people in positions that allowed them to embrace their own talents.

Yet another example involved Dave, a major account leader at a publicly held company. I was invited to help after members of Dave's team and other managers at the firm complained about his communication methods, including his abrupt leadership style. I interviewed several colleagues about Dave's leadership, relationship, and communication skills. He and

I then reviewed the results and made a series of goals for him that included developing a more empathetic approach to coworkers and leading more by influence than by making demands.

I had Dave select six work colleagues to give him supportive, honest, and timely feedback on his progress over the next four months. They started regularly stopping Dave after meetings or poking their heads in his office door to offer quick comments. That feedback gave Dave the encouragement and direction he needed. His communication skills improved rapidly, his team was much happier, and the company's CEO saw a real turnaround. At the end of the year, Dave was promoted to one of the company's key director roles. This time, I marveled at the amazing difference inviting advocates could make by simply offering supportive guidance.

As the years passed, I saw these kinds of dramatic results again and again.

Something magical happened when people asked solution-oriented questions, discovered and activated their natural talents, and invited the people who knew them best to make a difference in their lives. This was the Power of 3 at work.

The Power of 3

The real test of everything I'd learned, however, arrived with my cancer diagnosis. When the initial scan pointed to cancer, I indulged in a few hours of gloom and doom. The news was overwhelming. I shed some quiet tears as I began thinking through the possibility of dying, leaving Pam and the kids, and not getting to accomplish some dreams I still had. I soon understood I needed help meeting this challenge, and over time, my confidence grew. *I can do this*, I told myself. *With God and people on my side, I can beat this cancer.* Because I am a man of faith, the obvious steps were to turn to God, Pam, friends, and a host of medical personnel with lifesaving knowledge when I needed problem-solving, engagement, and encouragement.

The more I pondered all this, the more I understood that the strategies I'd used for two decades to help people turn around their businesses or personal lives were making all the difference for me.

Suddenly, as the saying goes, the shoe was on the other foot. It was my turn to apply the principles I'd passed on to others.

If I was going to overcome this deadly enemy of cancer and beat this adversity, it would take far more than luck and good medicine, as two of the cancers had no cure. No, the combination of these three action principles I had been using with my clients were the key to my needed miracle. The strength of the triangle is founded on the truths I call the "Power of 3":

- *Ask* the right questions.
- *Activate* my God-given gifts.
- Invite *advocates* into my life.

Within hours of my diagnosis, I began putting the principles that had been effective in my consulting work into practice. They shifted my perspective from overwhelmed to overcoming.

First, I needed to *ask the right questions*. I realized I needed to stop wondering, *Why me?* and instead ask, *What can I do right now that would be a positive step?* On occasion, that big *Why?* question crept back into my mind, like when I was flat in bed, immobilized by the nausea that can accompany chemotherapy. Or when my whole body ached from the cancer deep within my bones. Or when I was completely fatigued by the disease and drugs doing battle inside me. I found frequent reason to keep replacing unproductive questions with helpful ones.

Second, I needed to *activate my God-given gifts*. I knew that to beat an enemy as formidable as cancer, I would need to tap into my unique gifts. *Who am I?* I thought. *What personal strengths can I bring to this challenge?* I decided my natural optimism would be an important tool for generating positive self-talk and avoiding a downward spiral. I also knew I could make use of my competitive spirit, setting a goal of being healthy enough to attend my son's wedding.

Third, I needed to *invite advocates into my life.* I knew my own strength wouldn't be enough, and I needed other people if I was going to survive. I invited faith, family, and friends to come alongside me. In particular, I leaned on Pam as my rock. When she began researching lymphoma online, I allowed myself to feel encouraged as she learned more about what we were facing and how to combat it. And I made plans to relate my news to friends to enlist their support.

I also understood that this challenge would demand greater help than even my wife and others could give. I got on my knees and prayed, *Lord, help me. I feel totally humbled. I can't do this without you. Take me into your arms and show me how to get through this.* Talking to God renewed my sense of strength and peace.

> **Even as I absorbed the news of a horrific diagnosis, I realized I was uniquely positioned to get out of the ditch. I had knowledge and tools to get back on the highway.**

It felt like a revelation to see how each of these three principles worked in business and in my life. Equally eye-opening was how the *combination* of this triangle of points working together had such an impact on me and so many others.

Strength in Triangles

Picture a triangle, each of the three points equally vital to the whole and each connected to and strengthened by the others. It's no coincidence that the triangle is known as the strongest and most stable geometric shape. Engineers have long relied on the triangle in designing structures of every kind. The ancient pyramids, which have stood for thousands of years, were based on the shape of a triangle. The reason is simple: any added force is evenly distributed among each of the three sides.

Triangles make it possible for bridges to bear tremendous amounts of weight and safely transport us across water, a canyon, or a ravine. The three points of a triangle, strengthened by their connecting sides, work together to resist the otherwise devastating effects of earthquakes, wind, and floods. Triangular

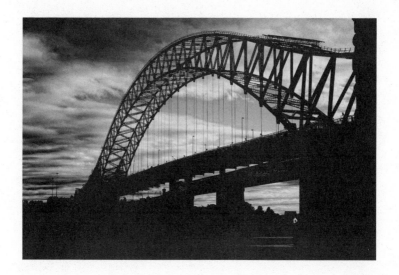

floor joists hold our houses together, and triangular trusses form a secure roof over our heads. Triangles are vital to our lives because they give us strength and shelter when we need it. The crazy thing is we don't usually see the importance of triangles, as they are somewhat out of sight—even though they can support our burdens when we experience challenges or problems.

This foundational power of three independent-yet-connected elements extends beyond the physical world. The Bible shows the Father, Son, and Holy Spirit connected in a supremely powerful holy alliance. And the number three is said to represent perfection or completion and figures prominently throughout Scripture.

The amazing connection and strength we find in the physical and spiritual realms is also reflected in the Power of 3 triangle. It can be summarized in three words: *ask*, *activate*, and *advocate*.

This was my long and winding path of discovering, testing, and living out the Power of 3 in every part of life.

My Promise to You

Wherever you are and whatever you face right now, the Power of 3 promises to provide clarity for decision making and confidence in the face of crisis. It's a unique, individualized, and comprehensive method for getting unstuck. It quickly pinpoints the areas holding you back and shows you the steps to take to move forward. It can transform the way you approach life.

This book provides a step-by-step guide to this practical and proven method that will help anyone, at any time, navigate the many trials of life.

In the chapters that follow, I'll explain more

about how you can put the Power of 3 to work in your life. Whether you're battling illness, developing your career, or navigating difficulties large or small, you'll get all the *what* and *how* you need to know. You'll gain an understanding of each part of the Power of 3 as well as important practical "power points" to help you quickly apply what you learn.

When you employ all three points of the Power of 3—*ask*, *activate*, and *advocate*—they reinforce each other, increasing their effect exponentially and moving you from overwhelmed to overcoming. In the end, as you live in the triangle, hope will light your path to success in every way. You'll know you can confidently face tomorrow, whatever it brings!

Practicing the Power of 3

At the end of each chapter of *The Power of 3*, I'll ask you a few questions to stir your thoughts *or provide a short summary for easy reflection and focus.* Find a place to write your answers where you won't lose track of what you're thinking and feeling along the way.

1. What trial are you going through today? Or what difficulties is a loved one facing?

2. What circumstance have you encountered that caused you to lose hope? How did you move forward? In what ways does that situation still make you feel stuck?

3. If you could wave a wand and make some part of your life better, what would it be? What does that new life look like?

4. Who can come along on this Power of 3 journey with you, so you can talk about it and encourage each other?

Free assessment: To see where you rank in the Power of 3 and how these principles might help you grow, I invite you to visit my website at RobbHiller.com to take the online assessment.

PART 1

The Power
of Asking

CHAPTER 2

Change Your Perspective: Ask the Right Questions

Keep your face always toward the sunshine—
and shadows will fall behind you.

WALT WHITMAN

I LOVE CHRISTMAS—every moment of it. Putting up lights. Decorating the tree. Eating cookies and lefse (a soft Norwegian potato flatbread rolled up with butter and sugar). Surprising my wife with a present. Sitting down with my family to a steaming, delicious turkey dinner. All of it delights me and makes Christmas my favorite time of the year. My daughter, Katie, enjoys Christmas too. Her love for the season began when she was a little girl, rushing to her stocking full of goodies on Christmas morning and picking up the wrapping paper after presents were hurriedly opened.

This last holiday season, however, wasn't so great for Katie, now a wife and mother of three active young boys. On Christmas Eve, my daughter stood in a church parking lot, her hands balled into fists. Though the weather was chilly, Katie was hot, dealing with multiple frustrations. For two years, she had suffered chronic pain in her left foot, and her insurance company had recently declined to cover surgery to fix the problem. Moreover, she was exhausted from spending all day preparing dinner for her and her husband's families. And her middle son, five-year-old Elliot, was still heartbroken after viewing the demise of a giraffe on a TV show earlier in the day.

Elliot was visibly upset throughout the church service the family had just attended. Now, as Katie and the rest of her family tried to hurry into their van and beat the crowd out of the parking lot, Elliot was melting down, flailing his body and refusing to get into his car seat.

I could see anger bubbling in Katie's head like hot water in a steaming kettle. *Why can't I just enjoy Christmas with my family? Why is my child making my life miserable?* The drive home was indeed miserable as Elliot whined and cried. Finally, Katie's frustration boiled over. She turned around, leaned over the seat, and shouted at Elliot, "Enough! I'm done with you! When we get home, you're going straight to your room with no dinner. I'll not have you at the table ruining Christmas for everyone!"

Back at the house, Katie's husband joined Elliot in his room and calmed him down. Just before the meal—thanks to a little encouragement from his dad—Elliot apologized to Katie. She accepted the apology and allowed Elliot to join the family for dinner, but her anger remained. She knew she needed to forgive Elliot, but she couldn't find a way past her frustration with the entire situation, including herself. *Why can't I be the calm, forgiving mom I want to be? What's wrong with me? How do I get past this and let go of my anger?* Katie was overcome by exasperation, guilt, and helplessness.

If you're a parent, you know just how Katie felt. Kids and other pressures repeatedly combine to test even the most loving and patient among us. They set off a physiological response and stir up our emotions, which often leads to a flurry of negative questions we ask others or ourselves. Unfortunately, these kinds of questions do little to help the situation and often make it worse. They warp our perspective, making us feel so bad about ourselves and our circumstances that we can't see a solution.

The good news is that we can change our perspective. We can cut off that physical and emotional response before it kicks in.

If we learn how to redirect our thinking in the first moments of challenge and crisis, we open ourselves to fresh insights and potential solutions we otherwise wouldn't have noticed. We can shift from a negative, closed-minded approach to a positive, open-minded viewpoint. And it has everything to do with the questions we ask.

Mad Dogs with Sharp Teeth

A stressful situation can trigger a cascade of hormones that produce dramatic physiological changes—the fight-or-flight response. That stressful situation can be environmental (like a vicious pit bull blocking your path) or psychological (such as persistent worry about losing your job). When that pit bull bares his teeth, your eyes and ears send a signal to the amygdala, the part of your brain that processes emotions. The amygdala takes over if it senses danger, hijacking your brain function.

If the amygdala perceives a threat—and a mad dog with sharp teeth definitely qualifies as a threat—it sends out a distress signal to the rest of the brain, triggering a host of reactions that prepare the body to act.

Allowing the emotional region of your brain to take over is a good thing if you're being confronted by an angry dog. It's not so good, however, if you're overreacting to a situation that calls instead for reason and analysis. If you're in a meeting and your boss remarks that your last report was late, your amygdala may perceive a threat—your job could be in jeopardy. But neither a fistfight with your boss nor your running out of the room are great career moves.

Many of us are even more prone to amygdala overreaction because of the destructive thoughts already running through our heads. Each of us has a set of messages, a mental running commentary, that plays repeatedly in our minds.

Too often the pattern of self-talk we've developed

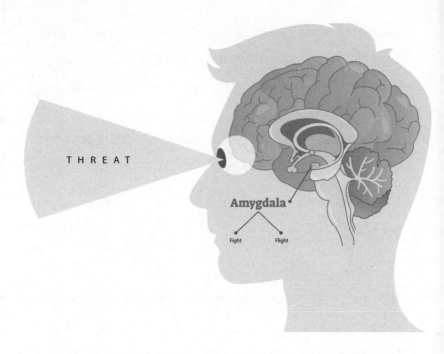

THREAT

Amygdala

Fight   Flight

is negative. We remember the negative things we were told as children by our parents, siblings, or teachers ("You'll never amount to anything.") and the negative reactions from other children that diminished how we felt about ourselves ("We don't want you on our team."). Through the years, these messages have played over and over in our minds, fueling feelings of anger, fear, guilt, and hopelessness.

When we confront a difficult situation—a boss who gives us too little time to finish a project, a spouse who's not listening to our needs and wants, or even frustration over the monotony of our daily routine—those negative messages often surface. Without realizing it, we ask ourselves questions that set us up for a fight-or-flight stress response: *Why is he so unreasonable and thinks only about himself? Why doesn't she respect me enough to talk to me first? Why don't I appreciate the life I have?*

Once we begin to adopt that familiar pattern, even a relatively mild provocation–such as an upset five-year-old who won't get into his car seat–is likely to trigger an amygdala hijacking.

Today's medical experts recommend a variety of methods to help reduce the stress that arises from fight-or-flight responses and negative self-talk. These include regular exercise and relaxation techniques such as meditation, deep breathing, and yoga. These methods can be helpful. But they don't go far enough. You need an approach that not only reduces your stress during challenging situations but also solves the problem confronting you—and quickly.

What if you could adopt a different perspective?

What if you could change your response to any challenge or difficult circumstance from the start? In other words, what if you could hijack the hijacker?

The Power of Asking the Right Questions

At the age of twenty-five, I was hired by Xerox, the country's dominant print and copy company, to join its sales team. My career began with six weeks of training in the Xerox branch location in the Twin Cities. They called our boot camp "Xeroid School" because it was Xerox on steroids. We learned all about xerography, products, speeds, paper types, and applications. At the end of six weeks, our manager assigned us to a small geographic area and gave us a test. Our task was to visit every business in our area and "sell them a Xerox copier."

I was confident as I set out to change the world, one copier at a time. I had studied hard and understood the Xerox line well. I was all pumped up with facts and figures, and I thought people would be eager to hear about all the amazing things my products could do. Boy, was I wrong. On one of my first calls, I introduced myself to the owner of a small business and quickly launched into my sales pitch: "This little Xerox 660 will take your original and make a plain paper copy that will look just like the original. You won't have to use that smelly paper from your other machine and see it fade over time." I offered my most winning smile and waited for the owner to ask for a contract.

Instead, he gave me a puzzled look and said, "How much is it?" When I told him the price of the machine and the supply costs, the man folded his arms. "No," he said, "I don't need to spend that much. Copies aren't that important to me. Thanks. Good day."

By that evening, I'd made twenty cold calls and had met nearly the same result each time. After a full day of failure, I was frustrated and dejected. *We've got a great product that does great things*, I thought. *Why isn't this working?*

Then Xerox flew me and my in-training colleagues to Leesburg, Virginia, where we were taught the heart of the company's sales philosophy. It wasn't about describing the benefits of Xerox copy machines at all—at least, not at first. Instead, our job was to first find out what the customer needed. If we had a product that matched what a customer was looking for, great. Now we had something to talk about. But instead of basing our approach on the idea of talking and selling, we were instead taught to ask questions and listen.

It made sense. I'd seen this as a kid when the Schwan's frozen food man visited our home. When he arrived, he didn't launch into a sales pitch to tell us about the newest dinners or desserts. Instead, he'd smile at my mom and ask, "What are your kids eating these days?" By asking a question, he learned right away whether there was a natural fit with his products.

I'd observed my mom use this method as well. At work, my dad was a leader—a director. His style was to tell us what to do. But Mom's approach was different. She asked questions. She might say, "Robb, what are you going to do for music this year?" If I said I was interested in guitar, she would ask, "What do you like about the guitar? How do you feel about the idea of taking guitar lessons?" In so many ways, Mom's approach seemed more effective. She gathered information that helped lead to informed decisions.

Perhaps even better, by asking and then listening to the answers, she communicated a sense of value and trust to the person she was talking with. It was a way to build relationships.

As I thought about all this during my Xerox training, I realized we were doing more than learning about a method for earning high sales marks. This was an approach for succeeding in life.

After my sales training, I returned to Minnesota feeling wiser, my confidence renewed.

I called on a man named Dick Wick, the new president of Burgess-Beckwith Publishing. Before, I might have found Dick intimidating—he was a big guy, six foot four, with a blond goatee. But now I had a method that was likely not only to make a sale but also to make a friend.

After introducing myself and settling into a plush leather chair in his office, I asked, "Dick, what are your hopes for this next year for your business?" He outlined several goals. A couple of minutes later, I followed up on Dick's answer. "What obstacles could keep you from getting there? How important are those issues? What are the implications if you don't make the right changes?"

I'd been in Dick's office for fifteen minutes and we hadn't talked about copiers at all, but I did have a good idea of what Dick wanted to accomplish in his business and how our products might help. My genuine interest in his company goals also helped form an initial layer of trust. When I shared how our new Xerox 9500 duplicating system would fix his production problems and actually save him money, he ordered one for immediate delivery. Dick became a long-term customer and a guy I enjoyed calling on.

Questions are powerful. They help gather information, lead to new insights, establish connections, and shift viewpoints.

What I've since discovered, however—in my sales career, in my time as an entrepreneur and CEO, in working with clients as a business consultant for more than twenty years, and in my personal life—is this:

To fully shift both our personal perspective and that of the people around us in a positive direction, we must ask the right questions.

Hijacking the Hijacker

The day my doctor called and told me I had a large mass in my abdomen, I was stunned. I had a second cancer. I would soon learn I had a third. Not surprisingly, my initial response to this dreadful news was disbelief mixed with a generous portion of "Why me?" *I can't believe it,* I thought. *What are the odds of me getting* another *cancer? Why is this happening to me? It isn't fair!*

A year earlier, I had watched my friend Mark's twenty-four-year-old daughter cry in her seat in the front row of a church. Kayla should have been one of the happiest people on the planet. She was getting married in just a few months. But she would do so without a father to walk her down the aisle. Mark had succumbed to lymphoma less than two months after the initial diagnosis, and this was his funeral. My heart was so heavy for her, her mom, and all their family.

At that moment, however, I wondered just how bad was *my* lymphoma? Was I headed down the same road as Mark? Would I live long enough to see my son get married in September? Would my wife still have a husband at the end of the year? As I contemplated a suddenly uncertain future, tears filled my eyes. My heart cried out, *Why, God, why?*

When I saw that death was not far away and felt the reality that I soon might not be here, I was devastated. Facing the sorrow of having to say goodbye to loved ones here on earth changes you. I knew that I'd be in heaven if I was called home, but I felt deep down that there was so much more life ahead.

My reaction to the doctor's call was understandable, even expected and normal. My amygdala perceived a threat—the possible end of my life—and did what it does naturally, hijacking my thoughts with questions that stirred up my emotions and raised my stress level.

But I had another option before me. I might have remembered that some questions put us on the path toward success and resolution, while others stop us in our tracks or, worse, do us great harm. Chief among the most potentially damaging questions are those that start with the little word *why*.

- *Why* **questions often come loaded with assumptions that might or might not be true.** For instance, if a work colleague walks by in the morning without saying hello, you might assume it's because of something you did or said. You may think, *Why doesn't she like me?* and be in a funk and ignore your coworker for the entire day. Yet it's possible that your colleague was simply distracted when you first encountered her.

- *Why* questions may subconsciously place us in the role of the victim. *Why is he against me? Why do these things keep happening to me?* When we allow ourselves to adopt this mindset, we're not actually seeking answers. Instead, we're trying to cope without engaging the problem at hand.

- *Why* questions often come across as accusatory, even to ourselves. When Katie asked herself, *Why can't I be the calm, forgiving mom I want to be? What is wrong with me?* she set herself up to be frustrated and dissatisfied with herself. All of the questions above fit easily into the category of negative self-talk.

Even though I knew all this on the day I first learned of my lymphoma diagnosis, my amygdala had its moment. But it didn't last long. By that evening, I realized I needed a different approach. If I wanted to beat this cancer, if I wanted to shift my perspective from overwhelmed to overcoming, I needed to ask myself a different set of questions.

> **Questions that begin with *why*, as in "Why me?" don't get us anywhere. But queries that rely on the power of *what* and *how* can change everything.**

What's the difference? I'd learned back in my Xerox sales training that *what* and *how* questions are practical and solution-oriented. They avoid the rabbit trail that *why* can lead us on, instead taking us where we want to go—a resolution to our problem. *What* and *how* questions allow us to hijack the hijacker. If you know you want to bake a cake, you don't waste time asking, "Why does it have to sit for thirty minutes in the oven?" Instead, you ask, "What are the ingredients?" and "How will I get what I don't have?" These are questions that move you forward and soon lead to a delicious dessert.[1]

In the case of my lymphoma diagnosis, I understood that I wasn't going to get an answer to *Why is this happening to me?* Even if I did, it wouldn't help me. What I wanted was an approach that would provide the best possible chance of survival while keeping me emotionally stable and hopeful. I needed to ask questions, but not just any questions. The *right* questions begin with *what* and *how* . . . but there is far more to the equation.

Discovery, Innovative, and Proactive Questions

One of the great benefits of the Power of 3 as an approach to resolving problems, making better decisions, and getting unstuck is that it works when you're facing a mundane challenge, a life-threatening crisis, or anything in between. Each point on the triangle—asking the right questions, activating our God-given gifts, and inviting advocates into our lives—connects to and reinforces the others. But asking the right questions is always a great place to start.

> **Asking the right questions helps us retake control of undesired emotions. It also quickly clarifies where we need to go.**

So how do you know the right questions to ask? The most useful right questions fall into three types: *discovery*, *innovative*, and *proactive* (DIP). The next time you're feeling intimidated by an important decision or crisis, you can *DIP* into your positive-response toolbox and rely on this checklist.

Many people instinctively understand the value of employing one or two of these question categories but fail to combine all three. If you want to ensure your best chance of success, however, make sure you explore them all. You may find it helpful to go in the order suggested here, but what's most important is integrating the questions and their answers. Like the Power of 3 itself, each of the DIP question types connects to and builds on the others.

Discovery
What have I learned from what is going on so far?

Innovative
What can I do right now to improve the situation?

Proactive
What could I do differently than I've done before that might lead to a better result?

Discovery Questions

Since emotions can so easily take us off course, discovery questions bring clarity to a challenge or crisis by helping us focus on the facts. Asking, "What is the core problem here?" helps immediately identify the primary issue. The question "What skills and resources do I possess that might be useful?" points toward a solution. Similarly, the questions "What will the impact be if I solve this problem? What will it be if I don't?" quickly demonstrate the significance of the issue and how much energy it deserves.

Almost as important, beginning a question with *what* frames our attitude—it means we're ready to learn and grow. In his book *Ignorance: How It Drives Science*, Stuart Firestein says that scientists' ability to embrace their ignorance is one of the keys to making new discoveries: "One good question can give rise to several layers of answers, can inspire decades-long searches for solutions, can generate whole new fields of inquiry, and can prompt changes in entrenched thinking."[2] Questions such as *What have I learned from what's going on so far?* and *What else should I consider before making any conclusions?* can lead to new, vital information that will help you solve your challenge or crisis.

Innovative Questions

Another reason we get stuck when facing a challenge is that we're too close to the matter. Chances are good that we could find a solution to our problem if only we could see it. Innovative questions, often starting with *what if,* enable us to see better. It's what inspired Walt Disney to ask himself, *What if this amusement park could be like a movie brought to life?* The key to innovation is changing the angle of your perception. If a dilemma has you stumped, try going for a walk. Move your body and let your imagination run with creative questions. Ask yourself, *How might I do things differently than I've done them before to get a better result? What if I actually tried what everyone says won't work?*

Proactive Questions

Feeling confused or overwhelmed paralyzes us. Sometimes even the tiniest step is enough to get us moving forward again. Proactive questions are solution-oriented and designed to generate momentum. If you've been unemployed for months, don't ask yourself, *Why can't I get a*

job? Even if your brain comes up with an answer, it tends to be a self-fulfilling prophecy. Instead, ask yourself questions that focus on turning things around: *What would I have to do to get a job in the next thirty days?* or *How can I make up for my lack of experience?* No matter what your dilemma is, a surefire starter question that will point you toward a solution is this one: *What one thing can I do right now to improve the situation?*

Working Together

On the day I received my lymphoma diagnosis, after realizing that everything depended on asking the right questions, I sat alone in my office and decided on a proactive response. I asked myself, *What one thing can I do right now to make things even a little bit better?* I looked out my window over the beautiful woods and wetlands outside. On my desk sat a pair of small polished stones I'd purchased years before. On one, emerald in color and slightly larger than the other, was inscribed the word *Faith.* On the other, a whitish river rock, was printed the word *Hope.*

I suddenly realized how desperately I needed both faith and hope. The answer to my question—the one thing I had to do at that moment—was to pray. "God," I said, my eyes filling with tears, "I don't understand the 'why' at this point, but I know you are faithful, and you are in control. I'm overwhelmed and don't know what to do. Please guide me right now. Bring encouragement to my heart and healing to this body. In faith I ask this. Amen." As soon as I finished, I felt a sense of peace that hadn't been there before.

My wife had been just as shaken as I was when I told her the news about my cancer. Both of us had cried a little. But now I was shifting my approach.

No more *Why me?* It was time to ask more right questions.

I'd already been proactive. Now I thought of discovery queries: *What are the most recent advances in non-Hodgkin lymphoma research? What are the most common treatments today, and what are their success rates?* Pam got online and started finding answers. The more we learned, the more encouraged I felt.

Pam and I certainly didn't solve my lymphoma crisis that first night.

We knew we had a long journey ahead of us. But I'd started to view my situation through a different lens. I felt I could beat this cancer. Asking the right questions had given me hope instead of leaving me feeling helpless.

My challenge was cancer. You have your own trials. It's inevitable that you'll come across trouble in your life—maybe several times a day! But you don't have to live in a state of constant stress. By employing the first point in the Power of 3 triangle—asking the right questions—you can take better control of your emotions, turn back an amygdala takeover, focus on the next step, and put yourself in position to find solutions to whatever obstacle blocks your way. It's a path toward reducing stress and gaining peace. And that's only the beginning.

Practicing the Power of 3

In the next chapter, we'll break down how asking the right questions (discovery, innovative, and proactive) can change your perspective and quickly guide you toward the solutions you need. You'll see how these vital tools will help you become known as a thoughtful leader and coach and as a curious person who is empathetic and understanding. This is a key first step in being influential, which all salespeople, parents, and leaders must be to be effective. Let's practice right now. Write down your answers to the following questions.

1. What challenge or stressful circumstance are you facing today?
2. **Discovery:** What is the core problem? What resources do you already have to help you solve it? What resources could you potentially acquire to add to your list?
3. **Innovative:** How could you approach this problem from a different angle? What are the first ideas that come to your mind, no matter how crazy they sound? What if you . . . ? (Fill in the blank.)
4. **Proactive:** Considering everything you've just learned through discovery and innovative questions, what three steps might move you toward a solution? What can you do now to make these steps a reality?

CHAPTER 3

DIP into Your Toolbox:
Change the Game

Those who keep speaking about the sun while walking under
a cloudy sky are messengers of hope, the true saints of our day.
HENRI J. M. NOUWEN

THE POWER OF 3 INVITES us to confidently face any
challenge or decision by first asking the right questions. When we confront a significant obstacle, our
natural first response is often to ask self-focused
questions of ourselves or others. A software engineer
thinks, *I earn a decent salary. Why do I have so much
trouble making ends meet?* A parent whose daughter
comes home with a speeding ticket asks, "Why were
you driving so fast?" It feels logical to seek the causes
or motivations behind an issue. But starting with *why*

usually isn't helpful and often is harmful. The answers we generate may be abstract and inaccurate. When others are involved, *why* comes across as an accusation, triggering a stress response and increasing the odds of a less-than-truthful answer.

> **Why focuses on the past and the problem rather than the future and the solution. Open-ended queries that start with *what*, *how*, *when*, and *where* are more likely to encourage thoughtful, even creative, responses.**

Like driving instructions or a recipe, open-ended questions move us to actions that immediately shift our focus toward where we want to be and what we want to accomplish. By the way, when we ask the right questions, we often answer our concerns about *why* and motivations along the way. And by centering our attention on open-ended questions and concrete actions, we generate momentum toward positive, attainable solutions. The results make us feel energized, inspired, and empowered.

Tools to Ask the Right Questions

Admittedly, it's difficult to avoid asking *why*. For most of us, it's our default! But as we catch ourselves about to ask *why* questions, we can choose a more positive response. We can DIP into a toolbox of right, useful questions:

- Discovery questions
- Innovative questions
- Proactive questions

This chapter will guide you in learning when and how to use DIP questions to address any situation and overcome whatever adversity you are facing. At the end of the chapter, a summary chart will help you apply these questions to your situation.

Discovery Questions: Identification, Information, Impact

Discovery questions are the first step toward getting us unstuck. They begin the process of specifically naming the problem or challenge ahead of us (identification), along with conducting an inventory of the resources we possess, as well as those we lack, for solving the issue (information). And they help us to determine the scope of the situation and how much of our energy to devote to solving it (impact).

Your DIP Tool	Goal of Questions	How to Start
Discovery Questions	• Gain clarity • Increase understanding • Stop confusion • Build trust	• Ask questions that start with *what* or *how*.

When I was a teenager, my dad owned a movie theater in our hometown of Marshall, a hub of southwestern Minnesota located two and a half hours from the Twin Cities. My dad sometimes took me along to the booking office in downtown Minneapolis where major film companies marketed their new films to theater owners.

In one instance, Dad and I sat in a big conference room waiting for a 20th Century Fox executive. A big man wearing a shirt embroidered with the Fox logo eventually appeared.

Dad was there to negotiate the release date for a promising new movie, *The Sound of Music* starring Julie Andrews. Fox had planned to premiere the movie in the Twin Cities and add theaters in outlying areas much later. Dad sensed the movie would be a huge hit, and he wanted it in Marshall on release day.

I listened closely as Dad asked the Fox executive a series of questions, starting with "What are your sales goals for the state of Minnesota?" That was a great discovery question. Get the facts out on the table!

The executive sat back in his chair. He grabbed a pencil and paper and did some math. After a bit, he turned to dad and gave him a big number that drew a smile from both men.

"How soon are you expecting to hit those numbers?" Dad asked next. He was forming an idea in his mind, but he needed accurate information to discern if it was even possible. I don't remember the man's response, but it seemed ambitious.

"How will you ever get to that number by opening at just a few theaters here in the Twin Cities?" Dad continued. The Fox man's response reeked of doubt.

My dad was a great businessman, and he immediately saw a window of opportunity. He asked, "How would you like to assure your studio that by adding the entire southwestern part of the state with Marshall, you will guarantee your success?"

Dad's biggest theater held more than seven hundred people, and he thought he could fill it most nights. Dad really wanted this potential blockbuster film, so he asked one final question: "Would seven hundred extra seats a night help you toward your goal?"

The conversation turned to negotiating terms of a contract, which came with the tough provision that the studio would keep 90 percent of the box office receipts for the first two weeks, along with an up-front payment of $10,000.

Dad had a deal.

My father told me on the way home that this would be the biggest hit ever. As it turned out, Marshall was the only outstate theater that opened with *The Sound of Music* at the same time as the big Minneapolis venues. The film became an all-time box office hit across the world. It won five Academy Awards, including Best Picture, and even today, it's one of the most beloved musical films ever produced. Dad's theater played this wonderful film not only one month, but an additional month plus, selling out every night. As one of the theater staff working for my dad, I saw the film fifty-two times, and I still get chills every time I hear the song "Climb Every Mountain."

I smile when I think about how my father used discovery questions to unearth key information about what mattered to the studio. Watching my dad showed me how to help people and organizations by acting on what he had long known: discovery questions can open the windows of heaven!

BUILD TRUST

In addition to gaining clarity, discovery questions lower defenses and build trust among everyone involved in a conversation.

Consider what happened when one of my kids came home with a D and an Incomplete on a report card. What was my *Father Knows Best* reply? I saw the bad grades and blurted out, "What in the heck is going on? Why did you get a D in one subject and an Incomplete in another?" I received a defensive response. "I didn't turn in some assignments and forgot to study for our big test. I just had too many things going on!"

Maybe you can relate.

Let's go back in time and examine what I'd say now using the Power of 3. My discovery questions might look like this: "What happened in these two classes? How do you feel about a D and an Incomplete? What are some of the consequences of not doing well in these classes? What steps do you want to take to move ahead?"

I wish I had fully understood this principle when my children were young. I would have been a better, more relaxed parent, and I could have avoided a lot of the unneeded stress that comes from raising kids. If I'd asked far more *how* and *what* questions, it would have been easier for my children to see me as a trusted ally. I know the tension in the house would have been diminished!

Asking discovery questions often helps us find common ground with those we disagree with, which is helpful in both work and personal relationships.

Whenever I tell my wife what I think she needs to do versus asking a question, it never works. Pam's response is usually seen in her face with a frowning eyebrow and tight lips saying silently, *Are you kidding?* Sometimes it is just a simple statement—"No." The same holds true in coaching or in sales. People don't want to be sold or told what to do; they want to sell themselves for the reasons that are important to them. Then they will be happy in their decision!

We might ask ourselves, *What is driving the other person's point of view? What is behind my view? What assumptions are we each operating under?* Michael Corning, a Microsoft engineer, says that a single question has often shifted his perspective when he faces conflict both at the office and at home: "What are the odds I'm wrong?"[1]

Finding common ground enables us to connect. When the aim is to connect with family, it may require asking questions together. Bruce Feiler, author of *The Secrets of Happy Families*, and his family improved communication at home by considering three questions together each week: "What went well in the family this past week? What could we do better? What things will we commit to working on in the coming week?"[2] By regularly affirming their mutual strengths and coming up with mutual goals, the Feilers developed a deeper bond and a shared vision for the future.

PRACTICE DISCOVERY QUESTIONS

Discovery questions are exceedingly powerful. As you frame your own questions, it's helpful to think of them in three key categories to take inventory of your situation and uncover the facts you need to move forward:

- **Identification** (What is the primary issue?)
- **Information** (What do I know about this problem? What additional information do I need? How have other people successfully dealt with this issue?)
- **Impact** (Why does this matter? What will happen if I can solve this problem? What will happen if I can't?)

Innovative Questions: Let Go of Limits

I saw the power of discovery questions during my dad's meeting with the Fox executive. He asked himself, *Is there a way to change this plan that will help Fox and also benefit our theater?* It led to this innovative question from my dad: "What if I could guarantee you an extra seven hundred seats a night?"

The next tool in your DIP toolbox is innovative questions. Innovative questions allow us to reexamine our challenges from a new perspective. Asking *What if?* leads to imagination and possibilities. It taps into our creative and intuitive sides—and often, what is in our hearts. It leads us away from being stuck. *What if?* questions often show us how to connect ideas and methods that at first don't seem to go together. Innovative questions move us from theory and brainstorming to practical and sometimes astounding results.

Your DIP Tool	Goal of Questions	How to Start
Innovative Questions	• Explore creative options for next step	• Ask questions that start with *what if, how, what, when,* and *where.* • Ask direct questions that open possibilities.

Innovative questions can begin with *how* as well, and they can also be direct questions where you are looking to encourage someone or find a new pathway of thinking or creative options to act on.

But the most powerful innovative questions begin with *What if?*

Jacqueline Novogratz worked for a nonprofit that made microloans to female entrepreneurs around the world. Her organization sent her to Africa, where she began imagining a venture fund that would back entrepreneurs trying to start new businesses, create jobs, and solve everyday problems in the developing world. Her idea was inspired by the question, "What if we could invest as a means and not as an end?" and has led her to a multitude of investors and successful projects.

Similarly, when San Francisco roommates Joe Gebbia and Brian Chesky worried about having enough funds to pay the rent, they put out three air mattresses and rented space in their apartment for a modest fee to out-of-towners visiting for a conference. Everyone enjoyed the experience. Then came their right question: "What if we could create this same experience in every major city?" It inspired them to form the online hospitality service Airbnb. Today, Gebbia and Chesky aren't exactly worried about scraping together rent money!

Innovative questions change your perspective. Just as important is their power to shift the perspective of the people around you. This is one of the most important ways to build your skills as a pacesetter, coach, influencer, and leader.

That was never more apparent to me than on an early morning shortly after my initial cancer diagnosis. I was wheeled into an operating room for surgery to remove lymph nodes from my neck and get a better understanding of the extent of my cancer. At this point I knew I had lymphoma—but how bad? How would we treat it? What were my chances of survival? The surgery would reveal the answers to all these questions.

Nobody enjoys being operated on. But I wanted this procedure done. *Now.* I needed to know what I was up against.

I was stretched out on a table being prepped, with a light shining down and three people hovering above me. A nurse inserted an IV, the anesthesiologist asked a few questions, and then we waited for the surgeon to arrive.

We continued waiting. And then we waited some more.

"It's unusual for the doctor to be late," one of the staff said. I sensed the surgical team growing uptight. Finally, thirty minutes later, the doctor rushed into the room. With worry etched on her face and tension in her voice, she apologized profusely and explained that her previous case had stretched far beyond what was expected.

I was concerned about my doctor. My situation was bad enough. I wasn't sure I wanted a rattled surgeon wielding sharp instruments on my neck. I thought, *What if I lifted the mood?* I decided it was time for an innovative question.

"Doctor," I said, "do you believe in God?" That caught her by surprise. With a thoughtful look, she replied, "Yes, I do." I smiled and said, "No worries here. My wife and I have already prayed that your gift will be used in a mighty way and that everything will turn out just the way it's supposed to: perfect. You'll do great." My surgeon's face transformed before my eyes. Grim tightness was replaced by relaxation. "Thank you so much," she said. "I know it will." The smiles on the other faces in the room told me the atmosphere had shifted for everyone—including me!—all because of the power of an innovative question that drew out a positive response and a sense of peace.

The power of asking innovative questions can't be overstated. It has the potential to turn negative attitudes into positive ones, both for you and for the people around you. It leads to relevant information and solutions instead of blaming. It opens doors to new paths when it seems you are stuck.

In my career, one of the first places I noticed the power of innovative questions was during leadership classes I conducted with an insurance firm. It started with discovery questions that helped staff identify a critical problem: their claims process involved too many steps and took too long, frustrating their clients and costing the firm's staff time and money.

Then I led them through a creative method that inspired new ideas. I asked innovative questions like these:

- What if we could cut our claims review cycle of twenty-two days down to six days?
- We could do this if we did . . . what?

These innovative questions and answers eventually allowed the company to cut the number of days in the claims process from twenty-two to six, reducing staff time significantly and eventually saving the company more than a million dollars over the following year.

PRACTICE INNOVATIVE QUESTIONS

You can do your own innovative-thinking exercise based on the process I've used with clients.

1. State your goal in the form of a question, like "We could improve our response time to customer complaints by 50 percent if we did what?"

2. Now continue by simply asking, "We can have happier customers if we increase our response time by 50 percent by doing what?" List all answers in a ten- to fifteen-minute time frame and keep listing any idea without judging the suggestion. From that list, pick the top five ideas that you like, and talk through the possibilities that have the potential to really solve the problem.

By using this process, you'll generate your own creative ideas for solving critical problems in your life and at work.

Proactive Questions: From Information to Action

Discovery questions provide information. Innovative questions lead to potential new approaches. Proactive questions enable us to apply what we've learned.

Your DIP Tool	Goal of Questions	How to Start
Proactive Questions	• Help you move ahead through thinking about actions • Reduce fear • Consider the outcomes you want	• Ask questions that start with *what*. • Ask direct questions that focus on concrete next steps.

Many people are natural researchers or creative thinkers. They love the process of gathering information and generating ideas. Only when they pursue questions that lead to action, however, will all of that information and all of those ideas be put to good use.

I've seen over and over that it's the combination of discovery, innovative, and proactive questions that leads to success.

THE POWER OF 3

Consider these examples:

- My dad's discovery and innovative questions during our meeting with the Fox executive led to practical, proactive questions about how they might implement Dad's idea for our theater to be included in the initial release of *The Sound of Music.*
- My response to my child's poor grades in two classes could have been different. After asking a few discovery and innovative questions, I could have followed up with proactive queries such as "How could you put your new plan in motion? What would be a logical first step to bring up your grades? Is there any way I can help?"
- Discovery and innovative questions revealed the insurance company's biggest problems with the slow claims process and possible solutions, but proactive questions identified which solutions were most practical and likely to succeed.

Proactive questions became immensely important as I battled cancer. As I started my first chemotherapy treatment, I had no idea what to expect.

I was led to a small, private room that had lots of bags of fluid and a big comfortable chair that could recline like a La-Z-Boy. Soon afterward a nurse inserted a large needle in my arm so that I could receive the five chemo drugs and reminded me that this first course could cause some side effects. The staff would monitor me closely, and I was told that if I felt lightheaded or had difficulty breathing to please let them know. I thought to myself, *What am I about to do?*

The nurse began the first chemo drug, and about an hour in, I felt lightheaded, and my throat was getting awfully tight. I immediately hit my red call button and shared with the nurse what I was experiencing. She slowed the flow of the drug, but it didn't help. She promised to call the doctor so she could give me a separate injection to counter the side effects happening in my body.

> **As we learn more information with discovery questions and ask innovative questions that can potentially lead to a better tomorrow, proactive questions are a wonderful tool to help us find practical steps we can take immediately.**

I asked myself a proactive question then: *What can I do right now to make my situation even a little bit better?* The only thing I could think of was praying that this remedy would work. You see, if my body resisted the chemo, I might not be able to take this treatment at all. At this point, I wanted the best chance of living, and the doctor said this was my best chance. So Pam and I asked God to help. Within fifteen minutes or so, I started to feel better, and my throat and breathing returned to normal.

By about three in the afternoon, I was tired of feeling weird and having one bag of chemo after the next. I began to ask myself the same question: *What can I do right now to help myself?* This led me to think of lying on my bed and looking up and out at the beautiful, sunny room that was vaulted and spacious. As I put my mind into that comforting space, the strange feeling subsided so I could continue.

The next proactive question came on the way home when Pam was driving. I began to feel nauseated, as my body didn't like what had been put into it. (Whose would?) As we went down the road, I simply responded to my own question of *What can I do right now?* I closed my eyes and began recalling the places and people that make me feel good. I did this for at least thirty minutes and apparently fell asleep. I woke up when we were almost to our home, and I felt a little bit better. I'd made it back home without getting sick in the car.

Here is a key point: when we face adversity, we seldom know what is going to happen next and what the outcome will be. We need to constantly remind ourselves to ask proactive questions because that action itself will most likely lead to a better outcome. That is why I wake up every day and say, "This is a great day that God has made. It is great to be alive. What can I do to make the most of it?"

PRACTICE PROACTIVE QUESTIONS

When you need to break free into a better place, ask yourself these simple questions:

1. What can I do right now with my challenge?
2. What are other options to consider?
3. What impact might this action have on helping me gain a sense of balance in my life?

Putting It Together

It's time for you to try putting these three types of questions together. Is there an area at work or at home that's been gnawing at you? I usually suggest to my students and clients that they start with discovery questions. Work through the questions below in regard to the challenge you're facing.

- What discovery questions could I ask? What parts of my situation do I need more clarity or understanding about? What information might give me a better scope of my situation?
- What innovative questions might I ask? What haven't I tried that might lead to a valuable solution?
- What proactive questions can I ask? What steps might help me move toward a solution? What actions can I take right now?

Sometimes it's more effective to rearrange the order of these questions, and sometimes moving once through the cycle isn't enough. The more complex the challenge, the more often the circle must continue as we go back to ask new discovery, innovative, and proactive questions on the journey toward solutions.

Your DIP Tool	Goal of Questions	How to Start
Discovery Questions	• Gain clarity • Increase understanding • Stop confusion • Build trust	• Ask questions that start with *what* or *how*.
Innovative Questions	• Explore creative options for next step	• Ask questions that start with *what if*, *how*, *what*, *when*, and *where*. • Ask questions that open possibilities.
Proactive Questions	• Help you move ahead through thinking about actions • Reduce fear • Consider the outcomes you want	• Ask questions that start with *what*. • Ask direct questions that focus on concrete next steps.

There's More for All of Us When We Use DIP Questions

In review, the process of asking the right questions from your DIP toolbox is immensely useful when confronting an immediate challenge, but it also offers much more. *It can be a guide for how to approach the rest of your life.*

Many of us are so consumed with getting to the next event or meeting the next deadline that we lose our long-range perspective. Or we're stuck in a drab routine that seems to stretch to the horizon. In either case, we're likely missing out on the future God designed us for.

Part of the problem may be that we're on a track that was decided for us. We've been influenced by the advice of family or friends or what we've read in a book or online. It may be time to slow down, step back, and ask some right questions: *Am I doing what I want to do? Is this taking me in a direction I'm excited about? What else intrigues me?* If you are a person of faith, you might ask God, *Is this the path you have in mind for me?* Author and consultant John Hagel suggests asking, "When I look back in five years, which of these options will make the better story?" As Hagel says, "No one ever regrets taking the path that leads to a better story."[3]

Your story as a better parent, spouse, friend, coach,

influencer, or leader begins by asking better questions. My clients share they find a real peace in doing so as they listen to the answers. You have heard the phrase, "People don't care how much you know until they know how much you care." It is so true. When we ask the right questions, we can foster trust and make better decisions.

As you move to the next chapter, practice this simple method today and see the positive results that come from caring enough to ask great questions. Go for it!

Practicing the Power of 3

Let's practice asking the right questions. Think of a situation you're facing right now where asking the right questions would be helpful. Then fill out the chart on the next page with some questions that will help you toward a solution.

My Situation:

My DIP Tool	Goal of Question	My Questions
Discovery Questions	• Gain clarity • Increase understanding • Stop confusion • Build trust	
Innovative Questions	• Explore creative options for next step	
Proactive Questions	• Help you move ahead through thinking about actions • Reduce fear • Consider the outcomes you want	

THE
POWER
OF 3

ACTIVATE

PART 2

The Power of Activating

CHAPTER 4

Step into Your Adventure: Activate Your God-Given Gifts

You must take personal responsibility. You cannot change the circumstances, the seasons, or the wind, but you can change yourself.

JIM ROHN

WHEN OUR CIRCUMSTANCES become a struggle, self-doubt and fear usually appear. These "happy zappers" leave our confidence on life support. As we saw in the last chapter, asking the right questions points us upward rather than downward.

Your next step in the Power of 3 reminds me of my family's first steps into a hotel we once stayed at. A greeter thrust open the oversize front door and welcomed us with a big smile. Then a sign in the lobby grabbed our attention: "Welcome to Your New

Adventure." Once settled in, we ventured out with expectation and excitement.

After you ask the right questions, the right next step depends on the type of support you need at the moment. If your child is struggling, you may want to *activate*, tapping into your ability of self-control as you talk to your son or daughter. Or you might seek an emotional uplift, calling upon an *advocate* to meet your crucial need to connect with your faith, your family, or a friend. Regardless of which step you take, living in the Power of 3 triangle will help make your situation an adventure so you aren't saying to yourself, *Why do I have to go through this?*

As I sat alone at home the day after my first all-day chemo treatment, my own next step—just to make it through the day and week—was to fully activate the talents God has given me. The challenge I faced was daunting and life-threatening. I knew it was okay to be realistic about what I faced and to feel down and discouraged at times. But the first talent I grabbed hold of was optimism.

Turning on positivity feels so unnatural when we're hurting. Why bother? Isn't it unhealthy to stuff our feelings inside? My approach wasn't to deny my feelings but to replace them with something better. In fact, I knew if I stayed in a depressed state, my illness and overall circumstances would only get worse.

In a moment, I'll explain more about the new science that demonstrates why optimism is so incredibly helpful. The chemicals from your brain—serotonin, oxytocin, dopamine, and gamma-aminobutyric acid—bring calm, peaceful, and positive feelings. It was the healthiest thing I could do to engage my optimistic nature and look for creative solutions to ease my immediate heartache!

Another natural trait I've displayed since I was a kid is an enjoyment of competition. I've always found fun in doing my best and seeing if I could win a race or beat par on a golf course. In my battle with cancer, I engaged my will to persevere and do what I could to beat this disease. I changed what I ate, for example, because nutrition was so important to the healing capacity of my body: more green vegetables, plant-based protein drinks, green tea, fish, and specific vitamins to help counteract the side effects of chemo. A lot had to change, and I accepted the challenge.

Those excruciating days I sat in the oncology treatment room, feeling the effects of multiple drugs injected into my system, weren't my first choice for a great time. Again, by choosing *activate* in the Power of 3 triangle, I lived out what I had coached others to do successfully.

> **Activate gave me the inspiration, practical thoughts, and solutions to make it through the day.**

Discovering Gifts

I first discovered the significance of natural gifts the summer before sixth grade. My dad was always looking for opportunities to teach my brothers and me the value of earning things in life, including money. One day we were at the store, and I saw a cool-looking toy truck I wanted. Dad simply replied in an upbeat voice that the way to get that truck would be to earn some money. I thought about it, and the next day I found an opportunity to do so. Without asking permission, I raided the family refrigerator and mixed as many cans of frozen lemonade as I could find into four pitchers of cold, sour satisfaction. I hauled my goods to the seventh hole at a nearby golf course and sold out in ninety minutes.

The summer heat still felt stifling later that evening when my dad came home from work. After rummaging in the fridge for something to drink, he bellowed, "What happened to all the lemonade?" Mom called back, "Just look in the freezer!" Dad hunted again and didn't see a single can. I don't know exactly why I came to mind, but he yelled for me to come down from my room. When he met me at the bottom of the steps, he asked, "Robby, where did all the lemonade go?"

"I sold it all," I replied sheepishly. "It was so hot, and I thought the golfers would love a cold glass of lemonade. They did!"

Dad agreed that was a pretty good idea, and I remember to this day the encouraging smile on his face. But that wasn't the end of the conversation. "That's great," Dad said. "Now I want to talk to you about 'cost of goods sold.'" Dad grinned as I forked over the cash. Paying for the lemonade out of the money I made was one of my dad's best lessons for me about doing business.

Years later as a freshman at St. Olaf College,

I needed spending money. Working at the cafeteria wasn't my first choice, so I began thinking about who I could help. Since I had worked at my dad's movie theater back home, I introduced myself to the owner of the only theater in town and offered to promote his movies to students on campus. My fee? Fifty movie passes per month, and I could sell the tickets for any price I wanted. He took me up on the offer on the spot, and every Monday I diligently walked the campus dorms and put up dozens of flyers for upcoming shows. The additional benefit was I had access to all the freshman girls' dorms and made many friends as I went up and down the halls. The theater's business increased exponentially, and for the next four years, I had a steady income.

I had a foolproof plan for selling the tickets. Knowing my flyers would drive students to the theater, I'd just show up a half hour before the Friday or Saturday night show, and there was always a long line for tickets. I simply offered those waiting in line the opportunity to buy a ticket for 25 cents less than the box office price. Before long, the tickets were gone, and my date and I could spend some of my earnings on pizza!

These incidents revealed two God-given gifts I still employ today: a bent for entrepreneurship and an aptitude for creative solutions. In both cases, I felt a deeply satisfying sense of accomplishment. These achievements gave me the confidence to develop my talents further, which led to my consulting career. When we activate our gifts, we step into our purpose.

> **Most people are hesitant to claim they have talents, much less name them out loud. You might wonder if you possess gifts, especially those that will help you live in the Power of 3. But it's all about doing what comes naturally.**

Doing What's Natural

Bentley, our twelve-year-old British Labrador, was born to love people. He makes people happy. When we take him for a stroll, Bentley inevitably attracts admirers. They walk over and say, "What a beautiful dog—can we pet him?" "What's his name?" "How old is he?" Bentley wags his tail back and forth and flashes a big doggy smile at everyone. He loves naturally. No training was ever needed. If a small child approaches him hesitantly, he's careful to be still and take in the petting and hugging without scaring the child away.

Pam and I were lunching with another couple after church one Sunday, enjoying our food outside on a large deck. Sitting at the next table was a family with three small children, ages probably five, three, and eighteen months. The older kids eyed Bentley and started whispering between themselves. Bentley smiled and wagged his tail. Suddenly the kids stood from their chairs and walked over to this happy friend. The little one hugged Bentley. After considerable squeezing and nuzzling, the five-year-old asked if she could walk him around the big deck. We laughed. "Of course!"

The kids giggled and squealed as they led Bentley around the deck. By now their parents had gotten up from their table and told the kids it was time to go. They walked Bentley back to us, and the family started toward the parking lot. After only a few steps, the mom turned and came back. She said, "We've really had a tough week, and this has been the first time the kids have smiled or laughed. Thank you for allowing Bentley to be with them. This made their week."

Bentley was just being Bentley. Bentley doesn't try to be a guard dog. He instinctively knows to lead with his best talent. In fact, if we tried to use Bentley as a guard dog, he would simply welcome a robber into our home and show him around with his tail wagging. If only humans were as good at understanding and activating their natural gifts!

Human beings also have natural talents. Take Shaun: he was a star sales representative for a company that manufactured medical devices. His sales numbers had begun to slip, and I was called in to work with him. After we spent time in the field together and I gave him some coaching, Shaun realized he was bored with the routine of his sales duties. His gifts included a competitive spirit and a love of new challenges. Shaun's true passions were helping people improve their lives, being creative, and being his own boss. So a month later, he resigned from the company, and today he owns and operates a yoga studio, where he coaches people on how to enhance their minds and bodies. He loves it because he's utilizing his God-given gifts every day.

When we activate our gifts, astonishing breakthroughs follow. We take another step toward discovering our purpose.

What's Going On: We Learn and Grow

Recent brain research shows how activating our God-given talents gives a true jump start toward making progress and gaining internal peace.

When we exercise the gifts and talents we're born with, we experience a burst of oxytocin that ups our enthusiasm, increases our energy, and helps us to be more positive. It makes us more efficient and productive and helps us to be better problem-solvers.

The amazing outcome when we *activate* is that we greatly increase our chances to succeed. We become better leaders, spouses, friends, parents, grandparents, and team members, and opportunities arise for far greater achievement.

The science of neurochemistry has helped us gain a better understanding of inner biological "conversations." Neurochemicals help the cells of our nervous systems "talk" with each other, similar to what happens when we get together with various friends. What's amazing is these neurochemicals coexist in various recipes as the fluids of the brain and other body parts organize their system's responses to stimuli. These neurochemicals are key in correlating our experiences, behaviors, and relationships. Their physical effects can be obvious. Just think back to what happened in your teen years when you saw someone attractive. Didn't that raise your heartbeat, tighten your muscles, and make your face flush red? Your voice might have even choked or cracked. That's how I felt when I first saw my wife, Pam!

We're at our best when our inner chemical mix matches the needs of our environment. What happens when problems arise and our internal responses don't fit what is happening around us? We feel undue stress. Our brain is flooded with cortisol and adrenaline—chemicals that produce defensiveness—rather than positive, connecting neurochemicals like dopamine, serotonin, and oxytocin. When the negative chemicals hit our nervous system, we lose our ability to have compassion, be curious, and cope. They negatively impact our memory and resilience, lower our immune system, and create inflammation. In many cases, we get physically sick with a cold, flu, or worse. Mentally, we dip or sink into depression, and our emotions wreak havoc on our relationships and our work. On the other hand, when we activate our gifts, we feel energized, happy, and ready to connect with the reality of life and make better decisions. Aligning with our purpose changes the chemical makeup within us, leading to healthier, more productive lives.

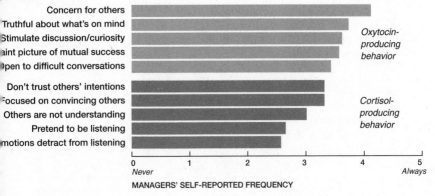

MANAGERS' POSITIVE AND NEGATIVE CONVERSATIONAL BEHAVIORS
They may be sending mixed messages.

BEHAVIORS

Concern for others — *Oxytocin-producing behavior*
Truthful about what's on mind
Stimulate discussion/curiosity
Paint picture of mutual success
Open to difficult conversations

Don't trust others' intentions — *Cortisol-producing behavior*
Focused on convincing others
Others are not understanding
Pretend to be listening
Emotions detract from listening

0 (Never) — 1 — 2 — 3 — 4 — 5 (Always)

MANAGERS' SELF-REPORTED FREQUENCY

What I Did to Activate

While each of us has innate God-given gifts, discovering those gifts isn't always easy, and while using the gifts may be natural, *activating* them—tapping them to their fullest potential—is often a process. Let me detail for you what I did to ACTIVATE my gifts during my cancer treatment and how activating made a huge difference for me even at my worst.

First, I *assessed* the reality of what I was facing to gain clarity. I needed to honestly grapple with the problem. In almost any situation, clear thinking is one of our best offensive strategies.

A — **ASSESS**
Know the reality to gain clarity of thought.

C — **CONTROL**
Self-awareness and self-control can be your best friends.

T — **TELL**
Tell yourself the truth and that you are not alone on this adventure.

I — **INVESTIGATE**
Be a seeker of relevant information to gain knowledge.

V — **VOICE**
Your feelings are real and need an outlet. Share with a trusted friend and let people in.

A — **ACT**
Act with confidence.

T — **TAKE OUT**
Take out your trash and forgive.

E — **EMBRACE**
Enthusiastically embrace the adventure that is in front of you. Good will come out of this as you live in the triangle!

In my complex situation, assessing the situation meant I needed to *investigate* the issues at hand—more on that in a moment. I needed to seek information, weigh options, make plans, and apply my best findings. This exploratory process allowed Pam and me to gain the wisdom we needed about treatment options and to prepare as best we could for the uncertain future. What is your reality in whatever you are dealing with?

I chose to *control* my responses. My immediate responses to the unknown of discovering these three cancers were fear and doubt—emotional, heartfelt, and normal reactions. But I refused to let the runaway negativity train carry me down the wrong track. I reminded myself that the gifts of self-awareness and self-control were key talents that I'd practiced over the years, and I used these abilities to their fullest. I simply determined to face each day, knowing there was no need to borrow trouble from the future. Self-awareness and self-control can be your best friends!

I needed to *tell* myself the truth. For starters, I reminded myself I wasn't alone. Thankfully, in my wife, Pam, I have one of the most loving spouses any person could ask for. I chose to recall that my family, good friends, church, and God really do care for me and that I have many strength-givers alongside me in this adventure. I continually recalled God's faithfulness in the various trials I'd previously faced. I prayed often, and it was amazing to see answers come in so many definite and different ways.

THE POWER OF 3

I *investigated* my situation. As I said, I assessed to gain clarity, but I needed to learn more. Both Pam and I are solution seekers. So we were off to the internet, our doctors, informational forums on leukemia, and conversations with successful patients to learn all we could about this incurable disease and how to improve my chances of survival.

On one particularly memorable ride to Mayo Clinic, Pam and I debated whether going through five months of chemo and a drug trial was truly my best choice. Wasn't there an easier option? We were on our way to an appointment with the hematologist, hoping for answers. As Pam and I talked, I got a call from our friend Bev, whose husband had gone through a bone marrow transplant a few years earlier, following the guidance of the same doctor I was seeing. Her husband, Brad, had not only survived but was back at work and doing well. "Robb and Pam," Bev said, "I'm so excited you're seeing the same hematologist we had. You have one of the best doctors in the field to take care of you, and you're going to do great with the treatment." She continued, "Robb, you're so strong, and I know you'll beat this cancer. I'm praying for you all."

We talked for a while more and then Bev said good-bye. Pam and I looked at each other, each concluding we had our answer regarding the path we should take. We were awed that our prayer was answered so directly and at just the right time.

I also seized opportunities to *voice* my thoughts and feelings. I let people in. As I explained the news to my kids and shared my real fears with a few close friends, I found that opening up about what I felt inside gave me perspective. My sharing also gave others a way to carry the weight of what I was dealing with, and their attentive listening and wise words helped reinforce my optimism.

I *acted* with confidence. For me, this involved remembering how faithful God had been in past trials. Like the time I was taking a small cruise boat from Sicily to Capri and we encountered a storm that rocked the boat back and forth like nothing I had ever experienced. I was scared. I got so sick that I passed out and began to slide off the deck into the sea, when a young man grabbed me and pulled me back up. I awoke hours later in the captain's bed as we were docking at the pier. They all explained what had happened, and the captain was quick to credit this newlywed as my hero. The young man and his wife helped me off the boat and brought me to the inn where they were staying. As I lay in bed that night, I gained a new confidence that God was with me no matter the circumstance. If God was with me then, he would be with me now.

I *took out* my trash. There's no need to hang on to past regrets, to store up offenses you suffer from others. It's trash that clutters your mind and heart. Undergoing an internal cleansing was a high priority for me. I knew any lingering unforgiveness would leave me a prisoner rather than the free man I wanted to be. Taking out the trash is essential to gaining clarity of thought. What time does your garbage hauler come each week? That's a good time to check your heart and consciously throw away your internal debris!

I *embraced* the fact that I had never asked for this significant challenge. Cancer isn't what I ordered for takeout, so to speak, but I chose to recognize the potential upside. Searching for lessons, benefits, and takeaways isn't easy, but it's tremendously helpful. I saw this challenge, for example, as fuel for reaching new goals in my life and career. It would help me strengthen my relationships, even the ones I considered already strong.

My logical mind told me that the testing I was enduring would eventually produce something more valuable in me, and I can honestly say that today I live a more joyful and happy life. I face most days with greater endurance, patience, and empathy toward others in trial. I have more gratitude and peace in my heart.

One of the facts we need to embrace is that we don't have all the facts. The trials we face almost always involve ambiguity—an uncertain journey culminating in an unknown outcome.

Embracing ambiguity means you can move forward even when you don't know exactly where you are going.

If that seems impossible, know that you can move forward with the Power of 3, tackling the daily irritations and agonies you face. When I found out I had cancer, I didn't know if I would live or die. But the process of living out the Power of 3 meant I was able to better deal with the difficulties and overcome the daily problems that were my new reality. I was determined to do battle even if I didn't know how the war would end.

Unexpected Gifts

A simple example of how my life changed was my appreciation for the nurse who took care of me over the five months of chemo. As she administered one drug after another, visit after visit, I made sure to connect with her and be optimistic. I did accept, sometimes reluctantly, that the adventure I was facing would lead to something significant. I just didn't know what that would be.

Recently, I returned to the oncology department at Mayo and showed the receptionist a photo of the nurse, my wife, and me on my last day of chemo. She saw the picture and ran to get my nurse. It had been a couple of years since my last treatment, and I wanted to say a heartfelt thank you to the nurse for all she did for me. I also thought it might make her day to see a patient who lived!

A few moments later, my nurse saw me in the waiting area and flashed the biggest smile ever. She sprinted over to me, and we embraced for a long time. We all shed tears. People who were once strangers, getting to know each other through adversity, were hugging like family. Without the terrible experience I went through, I would never have had that joyful bond.

Adversity can bring out blessings and help us become more grateful, tender, and understanding. I can now see this cancer as a true gift that God gave to me.

It reminds me of the words in James 1:12: "Blessed is the one who perseveres under trial because, having stood the test, that person will receive the crown of life."

The first picture on the next page is my last chemo treatment, with Pam at the far left, our wonderful nurse in the middle, and baldy Robb on the right. The other picture is two years later with my dear friend, the nurse who helped me through the ordeal.

You're reading this book as a direct result of this incredibly difficult adventure. Whatever your challenge is today, the process of recognizing and leaning on your unique personal abilities is key. Those

strengths are your best tools for succeeding in life. When you activate the unique talents you were created with, you step into your sweet spot—you step into your *purpose*.

It's like baseball. When the ball connects with the bat, *kaboom*! It flies toward the fence. That sweet sound of contact keeps a player stepping back up to the plate and training in the off-season. Or like a sculptor who can turn clay into the exact likeness of another person. The realism is jaw dropping, but the talent is honed over many years and many imperfect likenesses. Or like my college choral director who could take dozens of young voices in the St. Olaf choir and meld them into a perfectly tuned chorus of inspiration. His ability inspired us to work hard, correct ourselves, and achieve a sound that took us to performances at The Kennedy Center in Washington, DC, and the Dorothy Chandler Pavilion in Los Angeles. His natural talent helped us discover our own, but that didn't preclude the necessity of rehearsals. The results are so satisfying when we do something "naturally" and yet practice hard to perfect it.

Practicing the Power of 3

So, what about you? There's a secret to activating your God-given gifts. It happens when you

- know who you are,
- are who you are, and
- help others know and be who they are.

Let's see next how to do that by plugging into your gifts and helping others *become*. Here are some questions to ask yourself before we move on:

1. How well do I embrace ambiguity in my work and at home?
2. What have I learned from this chapter that might lead me to a next step in discovering my purpose?
3. What parts of the ACTIVATE acronym are important for me at this time to zero in on? What would be a next step?
4. What can I apply from the discussion in this chapter on how neurochemistry can impact my decisions and how I can better utilize my talents?

CHAPTER 5

Plug into Your Gifts:
Help Others Become

Be patient with yourself. Self-growth is tender;
it's holy ground. There's no greater investment.

STEPHEN COVEY

WHEN WE OPERATE IN AREAS where we're naturally gifted, we can't help feeling more energy, confidence, and optimism. Success breeds more success as momentum builds. But how do we identify the strengths we were born with?

Most of us have no idea what our top talents really are—or if we do know, we've drifted away from them. We spend the best hours of our lives at a job or some other pursuit. But many of us are in the wrong career altogether. One telling sign: a 2016 Gallup poll found that only 29 percent of Millennials feel engaged at their jobs.[1] My work with business executives has shown that of the five core areas that make up what is known as "emotional intelligence"—self-awareness, self-regulation, motivation, empathy, and social skills—it's often self-awareness that is most lacking. The key to self-awareness is understanding our personal strengths and weaknesses.

Let me give you a couple of ways you can recognize your God-given gifts and have confidence in your conclusions. I use similar methods with my clients all the time.

Asking the Right Questions

When your goal is to discover your gifts, once again, asking the right questions is a great place to start. Begin by writing down your answers to these questions, then look for common themes:

- What comes naturally to you?
- In what areas do you quickly get results?
- What brings you enjoyment in your everyday work and life?
- What causes your friends to say, "How did you figure that out so easily?"
- What did you most enjoy doing as a child and teenager?

That last question is especially critical. Searching your past often yields clues to your natural talents.

I was leading a development session for top-tier employees of a tech company. Midmorning, I invited each participant to turn to a team member and share what they did with their time when they were young—say, from age six to twelve. What did they love doing? How and where did they spend their time? What did they do the most back in the days when a ticking clock wasn't a concern?

After a few moments, I asked for volunteers to share what they had learned from their teammate. One leader played sports with neighborhood kids. Another mentioned a love of dance. Another had stories about volunteering. Then the chief technology officer spoke up and shared how his acute shyness as a child led him to build things. He had an Erector set—that classic toy of metal bars, gears, nuts, and bolts—and a battery-powered motor that could be assembled into an endless variety of tools, gadgets, and thingamajigs. The CTO loved coming up with new designs and solutions all by himself.

This leader's childhood interests led him to the job he occupied forty years later as a technology expert and brilliant inventor. And it explained the small Erector set in his office!

So think carefully about your answers to these questions, and especially what you did in your unoccupied hours as a kid. What do they reveal about the talents you were born with?

The Uplifting Circle

The uplifting circle exercise examines a situation by taking an all-encompassing look from various angles. As important as it is to explore our own perspective on our talents, we need to add in others' viewpoints to get a full picture.

Try this method I use with clients:

- First, list at least six people, preferably a mix of friends, colleagues, and family members who know you best.
- Then, write a short e-mail intro like this:

> Hey, friend. I'm reading a book about how to overcome life's inevitable adversities. It comes from the perspective of an executive

diagnosed with three deadly cancers. The way he made it through surgeries, chemo, and the daily difficulties of being so sick is called the "Power of 3." One part of the Power of 3 triangle talks about activating our talents whenever we face challenges. You know me, and I trust you. If you could take just a minute and reply to a few short questions, I'd be so grateful to have your perspective.

- Next, insert a short series of questions about the gifts your friend has observed in you:

  1. As you've gotten to know me, what natural talents have you seen in me?
  2. What gifts have you observed in me that are unique or surprising?
  3. How do you see these talents positively impacting others or my own life?
  4. Are there other ways you think I could put these natural talents to use? Any areas to activate?

THE POWER OF 3

5. Do you see anything in me that holds me
   back from making the most of my talents?
   If so, what do you see?

• Finally, if you want further clarification of a
  friend's response, follow up with a phone call.
  I believe you'll be greatly encouraged.

These insights will be a gift to you and will help
you better activate your talents.

> **Many people try to identify their strengths
> by their own observations. If you have
> limited your gifts discovery to your own
> vantage point, it's time to expand your view.**

Asking yourself good questions *and* inviting advocates through the uplifting circle exercise gives you
a far more effective way of discovering your natural
talents. Don't shortchange yourself!

Activating in Everyday Life

Knowing who you really are and becoming aware
of your true talents will help move you forward.

But following up with action is essential. As you move from knowing who you are to acting on that knowledge—*being* who you are, exercising the gifts you're born with—you'll enjoy new energy, peace, and encouragement.

The key is putting your gifts to use. Raw talent doesn't mean a thing if you don't take that swing. To achieve fulfillment in life, we must consistently *develop* our inborn talents.

As I was dealing with cancer, I took eight specific actions to activate my gifts. These small steps got me moving and created an environment where I could make the most of my gifts.

Below is an "Activation in Action" chart summarizing how you can initiate movement in a better direction even when you feel stuck.

- Start with any of the activation actions—the one that seems most relevant to your situation.
- Ask yourself and answer the activation questions.
- Choose a small, achievable goal you can take today—in the next few moments—to move forward. Don't wait; act!

ACTIVATION IN ACTION

	ACTIVATION ACTION	ACTIVATION QUESTIONS	ACTIVATION STEP
A	**ASSESS** Know the reality you face to gain clarity of thought.	How can I be honest today about my situation? What truths am I hiding from? What natural gift could I use to move forward?	Today I will . . .
C	**CONTROL** Self-awareness and self-control can be your best friends.	What am I trying to control that is beyond my control? What can I do that is within my reach? What natural gift could I use to move forward?	Today I will . . .
T	**TELL** Tell yourself the truth and that you are not alone in this adventure.	What negative thoughts am I letting into my mind? Who is along with me on this adventure? What natural gift could I use to move forward?	Today I will . . .
I	**INVESTIGATE** Be a seeker of relevant knowledge to gain information.	What do I need to know to thrive today? What unhelpful questions am I asking that are impossible to answer? What natural gift could I use to move forward?	Today I will . . .
V	**VOICE** Your feelings are real, and they need an outlet. Share with a trusted friend and let people in.	How am I letting people into my problem? Whom am I allowing to hear my deepest thoughts and feelings? What natural gift could I use to move forward?	Today I will . . .
A	**ACT** Act with confidence.	What have I accomplished so far in life? How can I use the lessons I learned to take a new step in the right direction? What natural gift could I use to move forward?	Today I will . . .
T	**TAKE OUT** Take out your trash and forgive.	What grudges am I hanging on to? How will I feel if I choose to forgive my offender and free myself? What natural gift could I use to move forward?	Today I will . . .
E	**EMBRACE** Enthusiastically embrace the adventure in front of you. Good will come out of this as you live in the triangle!	How can I turn this stage of my life into an adventure? How will I be stronger in the future because of what I'm doing now? What natural gift could I use to move forward?	Today I will . . .

These strategies are useful for activating in everyday life. They're also a perfect foundation for activating to overcome obstacles.

Activating to Overcome Obstacles

We all have an innate desire to use our gifts for the things that we're passionate about and that lead us to success. The difficult circumstances we face, however, leave us feeling like all our efforts are undone. Even if we're aware of the gifts we've been blessed with, something prevents us from activating them and moving into the next stage of our lives. That roadblock might be fear of change or failure, a negative attitude that drowns out hope, an unwillingness to be accountable for past mistakes, bitterness over past circumstances, or an unwillingness to forgive ourselves or others.

In my work with leaders, I've listened to countless individuals explain why they can't make progress in overcoming whatever issue concerns them. As their coach, I invariably ask what holds them back.

In the case of the founder of a tech company, it was ghosts from his past that stymied him. Mike was brilliant on the technical side but had difficulties with communication, meeting deadlines, and getting along with people. When employees disagreed with him, he often became defensive and lost his temper. On one trip to his company, I took Mike out for dinner. We talked long into the evening, and I learned that he had endured a painful childhood. His father criticized everything Mike did. It wasn't a surprise that when coworkers hinted they just perhaps might sort of disagree with him, old feelings of fear and rejection resurfaced.

All those reactions changed when Mike began by asking the right questions. He used personal reflection to identify and activate his gifts to deal with lifelong issues. He asked,

1. *What's my end goal?* For Mike, it was having happy customers and a profitable business so he could one day sell the company and enjoy retirement.

2. *What gifts and talents do I bring to the table each day?* Answering this question reminded Mike of how much he had already achieved

for his company through his technical brilliance. He could use his analytical skills to step into other people's shoes, see other viewpoints, and choose to respond thoughtfully rather than react in the moment.

3. *Do I expect to be great at all things? If not, does it make sense to work with people with different talents that might enhance my own?* Mike answered, "Of course not," to the first question and realized he could better use his personal gifts and accomplish his goals if he was more open to input and critique from his customers and employees. It was a long-term process, but the more Mike activated his talent, the easier it was for him to overcome his obstacles and step into his purpose.

Most of our struggles aren't wholly unique. In fact, others around us are very likely facing similar difficulties. We just do an exceptional job pretending that all is well. As I meet with people, I hear recurring themes, common reasons cited for not activating God-given talents. These are the difficulties that people think are keeping them stuck.

Consider these lists of common personal and workplace obstacles. Which of these examples resonate with your own life?

- Put an X in the second column ("That's me!") next to the obstacles that are most pressing.
- Use the third list to add other obstacles you face in these major areas or elsewhere.
- Leave the third column of each list ("What personal gifts can I use to overcome this obstacle? What questions do I need to ask?") blank for now. We'll come back to that in a moment.

FOUR COMMON PERSONAL OBSTACLES

Obstacle	That's me!	What personal gifts can I use to overcome this obstacle? What questions do I need to ask?
Health: "I just learned I have cancer or another health issue, and I'm trying to deal with all of this. Call me confused and fearful!"		
Kids: "One of my kids is having a tough time in school, and I don't feel I'm being a good parent, as he or she doesn't want to talk about what is going on. Call me doubting myself!"		
Family: "My husband or wife used to love taking walks, laughing, and going out for dinner. The connection and fun seems to have left our relationship. Call me sad!"		
Time for me: "I haven't taken the time to grow myself because I don't think I can spare it. Call me somewhat stunted!"		

FOUR COMMON WORK OBSTACLES

Obstacle	That's me!	What personal gifts can I use to overcome this obstacle? What questions do I need to ask?
Career: "I'm not really sure what my talents are, as I just do my job and wish for more satisfaction. Call me uncertain!"		
Complacency: "I think that not being sure of my talents makes me less enthusiastic to take risks. The job seems redundant and somewhat frustrating. Call me playing it safe!"		
Overwhelm: "My boss piles on work and expects me to get it all done regardless of the amount. Call me overwhelmed!"		
Leadership: "Many on my team are doing well, but there are several I just don't understand. I don't know how to motivate them to get it right. Call me frustrated!"		

YOUR OBSTACLES IN OTHER AREAS OF LIFE

Obstacle	That's me!	What personal gifts can I use to overcome this obstacle? What questions do I need to ask?

By taking that first step of identifying areas of focus, you will experience the joy of gaining clarity. Simply naming and facing your problems will help you feel unstuck.

So once you've clearly identified obstacles, what can you do about them? How can you make progress dealing with whatever issue, situation, or challenge is on your heart? How can you begin to overcome them right now?

Your next step is to recall the gifts you've discovered thus far and begin to consider how you can apply them to your situation. When you feel overwhelmed, these are your superpowers for fighting back!

Now go back to the lists and fill out that third column. Determine specific gifts you already possess that will help you overcome.

When you know your God-given gifts, you can take small steps to activate. You will gain momentum, and eventually you will see real progress.

When I was in the oncology treatment room enduring marathon sessions of toxic drug injections, I chose *activate* in the Power of 3 triangle. I had to live out moment by moment what I had coached others to do successfully, focusing on the talents God has given me. Pushing the "activate" button in small ways gave me the inspiration, practical thoughts, and solutions to make it through the day.

One way I did this was tapping into my natural gift for optimism. I usually arrived at the Mayo Clinic to start the infusion of chemo at 7 a.m. and left at 5 p.m. Once the first chemo drug was started in my vein, I would start feeling out of kilter, a little buzzed and with some tightness in my throat and chest. This would go on for a couple of hours, and then the other drugs were put into my system one by one. Sometimes my face would flush red; other times it felt normal. But overall I did not feel good.

While this was going on, I would close my eyes and think of each vacation Pam and I had gone on. Replaying our good times and special memories provided me with optimism and hope. One of my favorite times was the day we saw Windsor Castle in England. After we left, we ate at a small pub with a real fireplace going. The memory of tasting the pub's desserts kept my mind occupied with positive thoughts. I remembered another time, when we were walking into a quaint bakery in Paris, where we could actually use our French to order and enjoy a chocolate éclair. These memories helped me focus on the future by living in the past. The chemo drugs were forgotten for a time. Optimism, using the past to overcome the present, choosing hope versus the pain of the moment, and my faith in God were the keys to living through a day of chemo.

There were also bigger breakthroughs that came from deploying my gifts. One of my most amazing experiences of activating my gifts came during the brief few days between chemo sessions when I felt a little bit better. A client asked me to do a leadership session for a small group. At first, the idea sounded crazy. But the invitation itself lifted me up, knowing I could still use my gifts with as much strength as I could muster. I had to choose the right day in the chemo cycle. It required lots of extra rest and preparation. At the same time, it was incredibly motivating to me. It brought out my God-given gifts and reminded me of how it felt to do something I loved. The all-day session went well and reminded me how lucky I was to get to do what I do. I honestly didn't know if the session would be my last—if I'd even live to do more.

But knowing that, I sure was grateful for the opportunity. I treated the day with the care and reverence it deserved.

Help Others to Know and Be Who They Are

Using our gifts isn't a solo act. Our natural talents aren't given to us only for our own enjoyment. One of the greatest joys in life is using our gifts in order to allow others to express theirs.

After months of treatment and sitting home on the couch feeling crummy, I looked out the window at a warm, sunny Minnesota afternoon. I was feeling down because it was the time of year for making the most of outdoor activities. I'd have much preferred to play golf or sit on the beach, but now those weren't options for me. My doctors warned me not to touch everyday things like grass, dirt, or even a golf ball. Never. Coming in contact with germs and chemicals would devastate me. I had no immune system to fight off any potential invader.

I was also feeling down because Pam was out with a friend for the afternoon. I understood she needed to keep up some semblance of a normal life. I was home alone but knew it would be good for me to reach out to someone. Activating my natural optimism, I called to offer encouragement to a friend.

I called up Roger and asked how he was doing. "Great," he said. He immediately turned the conversation back to me and said, "Hey, Robb, you're the one who's so sick. How are you?" I shared my recent blood results—they weren't good—and lamented that I couldn't go out. Roger heard the despondency in my voice and said, "How about I come over for a bit and see you?"

I replied, "But, Roger, aren't you at work? I don't want you to feel like you need to leave just because of me." He quickly replied, "No problem! I'll be over in fifteen minutes." I got tears in my eyes as I hung up the phone. Wow! I was sick, and things weren't looking too good. And here was someone that knew I needed help. I had reached out, hoping to use one of my gifts to encourage *him*, and he responded with his own gift.

A few minutes later, Roger walked in the door as I lay on the couch. I really did want to lift him up, and I truly tried. But that day he shared my pain. He asked how I was really doing and just listened to me talk about the poor blood test and everything Pam and I had to do to stay free from germs. Knowing that an infection could easily overtake my immune system, every day was a battle.

Here's the thing: when we live into our purpose and activate our own gifts, we help others to do the same. And in this virtuous circle, we end up benefiting from multiplied gifts.

As a person of faith, I believe that God created each of us for unique reasons. One of my callings is to help people discover and use their talents. Yours might be to delight audiences as a performer, to teach children in a classroom, or to assist people with their taxes or in other financial matters. Whatever our purpose, we won't feel fully alive until we find and *activate* our God-given gifts—and use them to in some way benefit others.

The more we employ our gifts, the more likely it is that we'll help those around us discover and make use of their own talents and purpose.

Two strong VPs of sales that I worked with were Bryan and Ric. They were true activators. They clearly grew in activating their many talents over the years I worked with them. After spending time with their teams, I could quickly see each had extraordinary gifts in encouragement, leadership, and strategy. My goal was to let them see those talents by referring to their one-hundred-page leader's assessment and reminding them how strong they really were. Bryan could excite anyone by being his authentic self, and he knew how important it was to put the right talent in the right job and then let that person run. He did this and built another generation of leaders. My gifts helped Bryan develop his gifts, which in turn helped to develop the gifts of his team.

Ric had a unique gift. Ric would think out loud with me and come up with some of the best strategies I have ever seen. My role was to ask questions and encourage him when he was on the right track. When he was not, we just kept revisiting the idea, and something awesome would blossom like a beautiful flower. Again, my gifts of encouraging and building leaders helped Ric reach his full potential, which helped his team as well. Each of these leaders built incredible teams, a dynamic culture of accountability, and a strong revenue stream.

As you use your own unique gifts, look for opportunities to enable others to develop their talents.

- If you're an astute business manager, ask the right questions to get to know the passions and abilities of each member of your team so that you can put the right talent in the right job.
- If you're a parent, you can do the same with your children so you'll know how to encourage and develop their natural gifts.

It doesn't take an expert to guide others to their natural gifts. You only need to be willing to use your talents and to look for opportunities to help:

- If your gifts are empathy and inspiration, take time to sit down with people who are struggling, listen for clues to their inborn abilities, and encourage them in that direction.
- If you have a gift for resolving conflicts, ask yourself who might benefit from your intervention, allowing them the space to develop their own gifts.
- If your specialty is organization, you could help others reduce clutter and stress, providing more emotional capacity for them to explore their true selves.

The possibilities are limited only by your imagination.

To formalize this process, you can combine two points in the Power of 3 triangle. When you ask others the right discovery, innovative, and proactive questions, they will learn how to identify the most effective ways to use their natural talents, and you will have helped them discover their gifts.

The beauty of *activate* is we can all grow and overcome just by being more intentional.

Shortly after my first chemo treatment, I became very sick and had to be admitted to the hospital. As I lay in the hospital recovering, I was past asking questions. I needed human encouragement and some answers as to next steps for getting better. Things weren't looking good.

It happened one night with a lawyer who volunteered on Fairview Southdale Hospital's oncology floor. I was walking down the long corridor of the hospital dragging my IV, and I noticed a man sitting at the end of the hall with a guitar. As I finally made my way to him, I asked him what he was doing. He shared that he enjoys encouraging patients by playing his guitar for them. He could see I was sick, so he asked if I'd like to have him play a few songs. I told him I would.

I made the long trek back to my room pushing my IV cart, and soon he appeared. He played "Edelweiss," a song from *The Sound of Music*. Despite my weakened and emotional state, I tried to sing with him. Our mutual love of music and the joy it brings reminded me just how much I had to live for. Here was a stranger activating his God-given gift, which encouraged me to revive my own. This was exactly what I needed at that moment. It happened because this man was willing to ask himself how he might use his natural talents to benefit others.

△

We've looked at *asking* the right questions and *activating* our God-given gifts. The last few chapters of this book will bring us full circle to overcoming the challenges we all face. We need to find and be *advocates*. This is the crucial third point of the Power of 3 triangle, and there is a direct relationship between gaining advocates and the speed and success you'll experience with any challenge or situation.

Practicing the Power of 3

Our successes and trials help us to both discover our talents and gifts and to lead us closer to our purpose if we *activate*. Use the following charts to help you think through your successes and trials.

1. Begin by listing your past successes, going back at least ten to fifteen years. What came naturally to you? Can you identify the specific gift or talent you used in each success? How did this lead to a step forward in your purpose? Here's an example using a story from chapter 4: I set up a lemonade stand to buy a toy truck when I was in sixth grade. What came naturally to me? I lived just off a golf course, and it was hot. I thought I could offer the golfers lemonade, and I knew how to make it. I took my wagon and set up a sign. I sold out in ninety minutes. Specific talents: I had a goal (goal setter), looked for a need (inquisitive), and took advantage of being close to the seventh hole (common-sense solutions). How did this lead to a step forward in my purpose? I love helping people find a

solution to something they need. It has been my life's work for the past twenty-five years.

Success	What came naturally to you? What gift or talent did you use in this success?	How did this success lead to a step forward in your purpose?

2. Now do the same by listing some of your trials in life. They help us see where we got offtrack and can teach us something more valuable

than gold. What trials or adversities have had a real impact on you? Can you identify the specific gift or talent that would have made a difference if you possessed it? What was the greatest lesson you learned from this trial?

Trial	What talent or gift would have made the difference in this adversity?	What was the greatest lesson you learned from this trial?

THE
POWER
OF 3

ADVOCATE

PART 3

The Power of Advocates

CHAPTER 6

Invite Advocates into Your Life:
Accept Support and Strength

People often say that motivation doesn't last.
Well, neither does bathing—that's why we recommend it daily.

ZIG ZIGLAR

NOT LONG AGO, I was asked by a medical device company to help an employee pull out of a slump. The organization has a great culture built by leaders who care about their people. They believe in developing advocates who can support one another. After being at the top of his field for several years, John was struggling.

Before I met John, I had him complete a series of leadership and talent assessments as well as an emotional intelligence tool. My goal was to see what might be causing his dip in results and consequent stress and to determine if he was open to personal development. If that was the case, we would enlist advocates, and I'd help him lay out a path to success with a specific "Foundations of Excellence" plan. His boss would join to help and support him along the way, and John would get additional help from me with targeted materials and follow-up.

When we met, John looked nervous. We sat down for breakfast and started by chatting about the traffic that morning. Then I asked a question to get us down to business: "What would you like to get out of our day together? I'm here to help!" It took an hour before John admitted that for a long time he had been trying to do things on his own. He had spurned his manager's suggestions. He had clammed up and become unresponsive, nodding his head to whatever his boss said and then doing what he himself wanted. John was open to my help, but he didn't feel he needed an advocate within the organization. John's boss and her boss are tremendous leaders, but John struggled to let these advocates in. Why?

We Need Help!

Do you ever push advocates away or neglect to seek out an advocate because you're so busy?

There's a bit of a lone wolf in all of us. We believe we have to make things happen— alone.

I used to be severely afflicted by this disease of "I'll handle it myself." Back in the days before GPS, I'd drive somewhere new and get confused along the way. But I hated to stop for directions. I said to myself, *I'll figure this out!* The trip took twice as long finding my way through trial and error as it could have if I'd stopped for directions. Today, I know better. I've discovered the joy of having an advocate, with Siri or my wife directing our trip. Advocates take the stress out of navigation!

Many organizations are discovering the importance of advocates. In the past, a significant portion of leaders thought soft skills were a waste. Many doctors and medical practitioners, for example, believed bedside manner was overrated. How things have changed! Today, the medical field actively surveys patients about doctors, staff, and their entire experience. Providers with a "let's speed this up" approach are coached to create a more holistic experience. And we can all go online for ratings of doctors and facilities to glean insights from previous patients.

Business leaders are also learning the dangers of not cultivating a strong culture in their departments, divisions, or companies. Potential employees hop over to Glassdoor.com and read what people inside the company are saying. Leaders who don't value advocates, teamwork, openness, putting the right talent in the right job, and making sure the values of the company are lived out suffer from high turnover and poor execution. On a broader scale, revenue eventually goes down, down, and down.

But what happens when a company encourages soft skills, teamwork, the development of individuals, and a compelling culture? What happens when an organization elevates those values? Employees are motivated. Customers pick up on the positive atmosphere. Results improve.

One of the most wonderful outcomes of having advocates in our lives and being advocates for others is the mental health benefits we open up. Inviting and being advocates increases the flow of the neurochemicals in our nervous system so they can better communicate with one another. Then we are motivated, happier, and clearer in our thoughts and everyday decisions.

> **It turns out that getting and giving help really is, as Zig Ziglar suggests, a lot like motivation and bathing. We need it every day!**

If advocates are so important, why do we find it so difficult to accept help? Let me suggest a few key reasons you might identify with:

1. *We believe it's a sign of weakness to need help.* While we might be unafraid to ask small, innocuous questions, we avoid bringing up big issues. We're afraid to let others into our world, fearing they will think poorly of us or use our vulnerability against us.
2. *We may not consciously understand that we are stiff-arming potential advocates.* Our defenses

of not engaging, making excuses, or avoiding
discussions make life seemingly safe.

3. *We haven't experienced the great joy of having
   advocates in our life.* If we rarely let others in,
   we're not able to see their necessity.

So how did John finally see his need and come
around to the idea of inviting advocates into his life?
Once John shared what he wanted to get out of our
time together, we ran through the assessment tools I
had sent him. He saw the incredible talents he had been
given. He wrote down his natural talents and made a
second list of thoughts and habits that might negatively
impact how he was doing his job. I saw John's amaze-
ment as we talked about the natural gifts he had and
what would happen if he used those more and grew in
just a few areas. He smiled, relaxed, and shook his head
as if to say, "Why didn't I see all this before?"

By the end of our day together, he gained clarity
in his thoughts, and we determined four key areas to
work on. We devised measurable ways for him to see
how he was progressing. The importance of having an

advocate and a supportive manager gave John hope and fresh motivation.

The bigger revelation for John came as he began to see the other key elements of the Power of 3. He saw how asking the right questions was key to his success both professionally and in his personal life. And he certainly connected with the analogy of my British Lab, Bentley, being such a natural. We never had to teach Bentley to love anyone and bring energy into a room. He just does that naturally. John now saw his natural talents in a different way and was eager to activate them.

When John's manager joined us for the last hour of our time together to review the development plan, I could see the load on John's shoulders lighten. He knew there were people in his camp ready to help him!

The Cure for Loneliness

According to US Senator Ben Sasse, author of *Them*, a growing consensus among psychiatrists, public health officials, and social scientists is that the number-one health crisis in America is loneliness. Many factors make us an increasingly isolated people:

- technology that encourages us to pursue "likes" rather than real relationships
- the loss of stable, close-knit neighborhood communities
- declining participation in social, service, and religious organizations
- politically driven, us-versus-them mindsets

The result is a national calamity. It's not a coincidence that life expectancy in the United States has been declining since 2016, the first drop in fifty years and the longest sustained decline in a century.[1]

More than ever, we need each other. Studies show that people with strong social relationships experience

- increased life span,
- faster recovery from stress,
- better health (one study found that college students reporting strong relationships were half as likely to catch the common cold),
- greater sense of identity and belonging,
- increased confidence, and
- a more positive outlook and better mental health.

In addition, I've observed in my personal life and my work with businesses and other organizations that people who develop close bonds with friends, family, colleagues, and mentors are the ones most likely to succeed, conquer challenges, and move ahead when they get stuck. It's as if these people have extra measures of resilience, strength, and wisdom that others do not—and in many ways, this is true.

We're wired by our Maker for deep relationships, a truth made clear in the Bible:

> Love one another. As I have loved you, so you must love one another.[2]

> Greater love has no one than this: to lay down one's life for one's friends.[3]

Those words affirm that we function best in life when we rely on each other.

Nevertheless, many of us struggle, like John, with independent streaks that cause us to resist drawing on others' strength. Culture encourages us to pull our own weight and lift ourselves up by our bootstraps.

We sing with Simon & Garfunkel, "I am a rock. I am an island." We celebrate the strong and independent, not the "weak" and "dependent." The motivations for our independence can range from pride of personal accomplishment (a good thing) to feeling embarrassed to ask for help (a bad thing).

There are additional intriguing words from the Bible that not only capture this dilemma but supply a perfect solution. A great leader wrote to his friends, "Carry each other's burdens."[4] A few lines later, however, this leader says, "Each one should carry their own load."[5]

What? Those two bits of advice seem confusing, if not contradictory. He seems to be saying, "Carry each other's burdens—but wait! You should pull your own weight."

The early readers of those words would have understood the real intent. The words *burden* and *load* seem like synonyms in English, but the words have very different meanings in the original Greek language. They're actually a vivid picture! The Greek word for *burden* is literally a boulder too big for one person to carry. *Load* in Greek is the word for a Roman soldier's daypack, the basic supplies and tools the warrior needed for battle.

> **In other words, it's good to be strong and take responsibility for yourself. But it's also absolutely necessary to know when to call for help when the burden is too great to bear alone.**

There's really no conflict between these two ideas. It's much like the points of the Power of 3 triangle. The first two are things we do for ourselves:

- *Ask* the right questions.
- *Activate* your God-given gifts.

But the third point involves others in our challenge:

- Invite *advocates* into your life.

Have you ever known someone who was "too needy" or "codependent," to use the pop psychology terms? Chances are you and that individual were struggling to find the right balance between standing on your own (carrying your own load of daily necessities) and relying on others (getting help with a burden that is too big to carry). What wisdom!

The Triangle within the Triangle

More than ever in today's complex and challenging world, we need to learn how to invite advocates into our lives. Our advocates can be divided into three categories—another triangle within the Power of 3 triangle: family, friends, and faith.

Family

Our families represent our earliest opportunity to be blessed by advocates. Ideally, parents and siblings show us the power and potential of what it means to have an advocate, setting a loving and positive tone for the rest of our lives. As I was growing up, everyone in my family fulfilled this role in one way or another, but especially my mom. Her continuing support, including her encouragement to pursue my musical gifts, was one of the pillars of my life.

Hopefully, our need for advocates is reinforced early and often as our world expands beyond home. For example, like many kids, I struggled with adjusting to junior high school. I had entered a scary new world and was unsure of myself. I was trying to find my identity. My parents, sensing my unease, encouraged me to take guitar lessons. They knew by this point that music was one of my gifts and that developing my skill would give me more confidence, and they were right. But my lessons with Don, a blind gentleman who taught me how to play, gave me even more. His encouragement and passion for attaining the perfect sound showed me that if I pushed myself,

I could achieve more than I realized. His ability to play great music on a beat-up acoustic guitar, without sight, demonstrated that obstacles can be overcome. Don showed me the importance of practice and discipline. He was one in a line of many valuable advocates to follow.

We need advocates because the moment we believe we can stand alone against the world's trials is the moment we are most vulnerable.

But talking about family advocates raises an important question: What if your family hasn't been supportive? Families aren't perfect . . . and neither are we! After evaluating and talking heart-to-heart with thousands of people in the past twenty-plus years, I have deep empathy and understanding when your only family support might be from a single parent, one sibling, or no one at all. We can grieve the loss or estrangement of family situations where things didn't turn out well. It's a process to accept that we didn't get what we needed from our family because they most likely experienced that same lack in their own past.

We might be able to reconcile some past differences with family, and it's worthwhile to try. Whatever the outcome of our reconciliation efforts, we still can invite and develop friends as advocates to fill the natural and God-given need we all have for support.

This is one of the most powerful parts of the Power of 3—inviting new advocates into our lives because we need others, and when we do, we can then reciprocate by being an advocate to them.

Friends and Coworkers

As we grow, of course, friends take on new importance in our social sphere. They can become our greatest allies—loved ones to celebrate and mourn with, sounding boards and guides through uncertain times, people willing to speak truth when we're blind to our own mistakes.

Several friends I gained in college have remained close in the decades since. Likewise, I now cherish several clients as good friends. These comrades give me invaluable companionship, encouragement, advice, and support, never more so than when I was being treated for cancer. I don't know if I could have gotten through those days without them.

Though I've been fortunate with my friendships, many men struggle to establish long-term relationships. Men are much more likely than women to go it alone when facing a trial. Unfortunately, that attitude can be costly. We—both men and women—*must* cultivate connections to succeed in life.

Hopefully by now you feel a nudge to reconnect with friends and perhaps casual acquaintances you enjoyed but never worked to develop a friendship with. In my church, service organization groups like Rotary, my gym, my workplace, and even friends of my kids, I've found friends that can turn into advocates.

When I began to let people know my devastating news of three cancers, I found an incredible number of advocates. One of the most touching advocates was Sherman Black, a CEO who immediately called and volunteered to take me down to the Mayo Clinic. I had helped Sherman with his company in the past, and we had developed a friendship due to our kids being in high school together. He called me weekly for five months. I was touched by another CEO, Jerry Mattys, who when he learned of my situation, said, "Robb, you've helped us and been on our schedule for the past ten years. We are now on yours. You let us know how you are doing and what you can do, and that will be just perfect."

I admit, the many responses like this still make me tear up today. Advocates make life meaningful. So, who do you need to call today and get together with for a cup of coffee?

Faith

The final point in the triangle within the triangle is faith. It's the foundation of my life, as well as of the Power of 3.

> When we tap into a wellspring of strength and wisdom much greater than ourselves, we find the resources we need to meet any challenge and to bring meaning to our existence.

Time magazine reports that

study after study has found that religious people tend to be less depressed and less anxious than nonbelievers, better able to handle the vicissitudes of life than nonbelievers. A 2015 survey by

researchers at the London School of Economics
and the Erasmus University Medical Center
in the Netherlands found that participating
in a religious organization was the only social
activity associated with sustained happiness—
even more than volunteering for a charity,
taking educational courses or participating in
a political or community organization.[6]

I've observed this same outcome among friends, colleagues, and clients. It's certainly been true of my own journey.

What does brain research say about meditation and prayer? Neuroscientists have discovered that prayerful meditation slows you down and helps you become more aware of your breathing, auditory listening, and the sensory prefrontal cortex of your brain. When we prayerfully meditate, we have more gray matter available, which is linked to decision making and working memory. What I find amazing is that people who do this regularly have the same gray matter in their prefrontal cortex as people half their age.[7] That's great news for all of us over fifty!

The science behind this is simple yet profound. Of a study done by neuroscientist Sara Lazar of the Harvard Medical School, those that meditated over eight weeks at an average of twenty-seven minutes a day saw a shrinkage of their amygdala. This is the part of the brain that can send us into a tizzy if we aren't careful, and it is where anxiety, stress, and aggression come from.[8]

Adversity often shakes our faith, sometimes to its foundations. When you most feel a need for faith, you might have very little of it! The unique part of this triangle is that you don't need much faith at all—it can be as small as a mustard seed but still be powerful. The Bible points out that this mustard seed of faith can be the foundation to support and strengthen us as we carry out whatever situation or role we are in each day.

I've found my Christian faith to be indispensable not only in facing cancer but in finding my way through all of life. What does faith mean to you? What do you trust? What truths are foundational to your life? Whether or not you identify with an organized religion, your faith likely includes beliefs, decisions, commitments, even shoulds and shouldn'ts that support and guide you. Faith involves things you might not be able to prove to a skeptic, but to you, their reality is beyond doubt. Faith can lift you up "on eagle's wings," as one contemporary hymn puts it.

The Power of 3 relies on the power of the triangle, that geometric shape that can hold large loads without collapsing or changing shape. I've found that the greatest triangle of all is the Trinity—Father, Son, and Holy Spirit—the undergirding reality of the Christian faith.

The triangle of the Trinity is free to all, and there is no wait. In this triangle, we have access to the power of the Trinity through prayer.

An Advocate at the Emergency Room

I learned the importance of inviting advocates during the whole of my cancer experience, but there was a time at the beginning of chemo treatments when this was particularly apparent. I had just finished my first all-day chemo session, and I walked out of Mayo Clinic in a daze. Home was a miserable hour and a half drive away, and I felt nauseous for most of the drive.

I was okay for the first week afterward, but when my

follow-up meds changed, my body began to painfully react to the chemotherapy. Another day later, I knew something wasn't right. The pain was getting stronger. I could feel it in my bones—aching . . . throbbing . . . unrelenting. It grew in intensity as though I were baking outside in a hot July sun. The nausea was also increasing.

I tried the medications the doctor gave me. Nothing worked. I tried sleeping but couldn't. The pain was so bad, I was in the fetal position. I tried watching TV as a distraction, but I couldn't get my mind off my pain. The evening wore on with no relief.

While I writhed in pain, Pam called my doctors for advice. I hadn't eaten or drunk much in two days. The doctor wrote a new prescription. While I lay on the couch, Pam researched everything she could about my symptoms online and offered what encouragement she could.

I felt helpless as the hours passed in slow motion—10 p.m. . . . 11 p.m. . . . 12 a.m. . . .

At 1 a.m., Pam, who now felt as powerless as I did, decided we'd had enough. "That's it," she announced. "We're getting you to the ER."

We left in a rush. Pam usually fastidiously follows the rules of the road, but this time she zipped past cars on the highway, sped along side streets, and aggressively rolled through stop signs.

We arrived at the ER, checked in, and were quickly ushered into an exam room. My pain had grown far worse. My entire body felt like one massive aching tooth, times twenty, coupled with severe nausea. I wish I could have described my pain to the nurse, but I was growing incoherent. My face said it all.

Before long, a friendly doctor entered and instructed the nurse to give me a shot of morphine. Before I could get that beautiful painkiller, however, they needed to do blood work and administer a series of tests.

We waited and waited for the tech to get started. I didn't understand why they weren't fixing the pain. I wanted relief. Finally, the IV went in and vials of blood were sucked out of my system. Even in my incoherence, I felt like saying, "Can't we just stop the pain?"

Once they had taken my blood, the nurse returned to my ER room with the morphine. I started to feel "happy" as the pain slowly subsided.

After more tests and analysis, the ER team gave me

another pain med and sent me home. They had ruled out other causes of my pain and sickness and thought I would rebound back to a somewhat normal state— normal, that is, considering the chemo making its way through my body.

The next night, however, I was back in the same ER with all the same symptoms. I was still in pain. I was nauseous. Eating or drinking felt impossible. After we repeated the exact same routine as the previous night, they admitted me to the hospital and put me in a general room. Strong morphine-type drugs weren't helping. We were nowhere close to discovering the real cause of all the symptoms and what to do about it.

Over the next few days, I saw numerous doctors. Nothing changed. The pain was still there, and I felt hideously bad.

My son Ryan visited; my daughter, Katie, called from California; my eldest son, Rick, called; good friends stopped by; and my sister-in-law Nan brought a teddy bear. They all encouraged me to keep going. I barely responded. I still wasn't eating, still felt nauseous, and still felt pain deep in my bones. I was lethargic and discouraged.

What I didn't know was that I was starting to slip away—physically, mentally, and spiritually. I was drained and had no hope or energy to fight back. How could I combat this pain if I didn't know what was causing it? My normally positive and determined disposition fell, slowly succumbing to my physical conditions. Months later, Pam told me she could see I was losing the will to live.

Thankfully, the doctors could also plainly see that I wasn't doing well, and they moved me again.

I was now in the oncology ward. The hospital doctors grasped that I was struggling but were puzzled by my symptoms and how to help. They tried different combinations of medicine without making progress.

By day four, my pain was unbearable. Not even morphine helped. I just felt awful.

The emotional and spiritual torment Pam was experiencing finally got to be too much for her. Her courageous hope began to fade. A dam of tears threatened to burst, and she hurriedly left the room. She had to do something.

Pam sought an advocate.

Pam saw a nurse in the hallway and quickly walked

over to her. Pam introduced herself and said, "My husband needs help. Nothing has been working these past few days. We need help."

The Fairview Southdale nurse—Susan—listened to Pam and studied my chart. "I'm going to talk to a doctor," she said, "but I'll be back soon." She took a step, paused, and then turned back to Pam. "I understand how you are feeling right now. Oncology is my specialty, and I've done this for thirty-five years. We're going to figure this out. Trust me."

Those words made their way into Pam's spirit and revived her diminishing hope. Pam knew Susan had heard us. She thought, *I've found someone with real expertise who will help us.*

Soon after, Susan came back with the floor's oncology doctor. He looked at all my charts. He asked me several questions, paused, and looked up.

"Susan," he said, "run to the pharmacy and get Claritin for his pain." With his signed order, Susan rushed off.

The doctor turned to Pam and me and said, "If this works, Robb will start feeling better within an hour.

Then we can put him on a schedule to help him through his chemo and trial drug. I'll be back to check on him."

An oncology doctor who constantly dealt in life and death prescribed a common allergy pill for my pain? I couldn't believe it.

My first thought was, *Why should this work? Nothing else has.* But somehow hope worked its way in. *What do we have to lose?* I remember praying, *Lord, please let this work.*

I know this is hard to believe, but within a few hours, I started to notice a difference. The pain eased. I felt so much better by late afternoon, and a day and a half later, I was eating again with no pain and no nausea. I was well enough to be discharged and so grateful to be going back home.

Pam saw me losing the will to live, and neither of us knew what to do. We were both at the end of our ropes. But instead of losing hope, Pam sought an advocate at just the right time. And in this case, it was the difference between death and life.

Not all situations are life-or-death, but I guarantee that your life will be improved as you open the door to the advocates of family, friends, and faith around you. In the next chapter, we'll look at effective ways to invite—and be—advocates.

Practicing the Power of 3

It turns out that getting and giving help is, as Zig Ziglar says, a lot like motivation and bathing—we need it every day! Think through the following questions:

1. Who are your trusted friends that you can call at three in the morning and know they would be there for you? And in your family, who are your trusted advocates? How does this impact you today?
2. How often are you reaching out to develop advocates at work and in everyday life? Is there an opportunity here to strengthen your triangle?
3. Who do you need to call today to schedule a time to meet?
4. Is your faith helping you grow each day? If not to the extent you desire, what might be a next step to grow in this area of your life?

5. Last, since it is also vital to be an advocate to others, who could you encourage and help while expecting nothing in return?

CHAPTER 7

Cultivate Life-Giving Connections: Lean On Family, Friends, and Faith

To solve any problem, here are three questions to ask yourself: First, what could I do? Second, what could I read? And third, who could I ask?

JIM ROHN

As I was growing up, my dad taught me many life skills, but he was especially intentional about mentoring me in business. My dad took over the movie theater business in small-town Marshall, Minnesota, when I was just ten years old. The theater where I first saw *The Sound of Music* was a seven-hundred-seat venue in a town of fewer than seven thousand! My dad also owned an outdoor drive-in movie theater big enough for a couple hundred cars. Yes, people would load up the family and sit in their car to watch a movie. If they had a pickup truck or station wagon, they would pull in backward and let the kids hang out the tailgate. Of course, the drive-in was also a place to take a date. Hopefully she would slide over next to you as you watched John Wayne take on the bad guys.

My dad gave me the worst jobs at the drive-in, like cleaning the concession stand and scrubbing toilets. What was sometimes worst of all was picking up the litter the morning after a showing. What lessons! And all for the take-home pay of $1.25 an hour. Dad put the rest of my pay into a savings account, teaching me the value of saving for my future whether I liked it or not.

When I was a high school sophomore, I overheard my dad complaining about declining concession sales at the drive-in. It didn't take long for my head to start popping with ideas for increasing sales. The concession stand was a large walk-in affair, like a long cafeteria-style service where you could grab what you wanted and pay at the end. My friends made fun of the dreary, dated interior, and they wondered why getting a Coney dog was such an ordeal.

I asked dad if he wanted to hear my suggestions,

and it turned out he wanted more than what I could come up with off the top of my head. He sent me to the town's new library to study industry trends and instructed me to present my thoughts on paper. I thought it was odd for a fifteen-year-old to put together something Dad called a business plan. Little did I know that he was using his schooling and experience to teach me the rudiments of business.

I grabbed a fresh tablet and multiple colored pens. The librarian taught me how to do research, an invaluable process when I started college. One of my big findings? Painting the concession stand in bold oranges and yellows would encourage people to eat and drink more.

My report so enthused my dad that he gave the go-ahead on all my ideas, with one major condition. It was up to me to do all the ordering, rearranging, and painting. The sales register kept ringing up and up, and by the end of the season, it was clear my ideas had worked. Putting large tubs of buttered popcorn up front and moving little boxes to the back was a game changer. Soda sales shot up too. My one dud idea was preloading the Coney dogs with the customary barbecue sauce and setting them out ahead of time. The buns turned to mush and had to be tossed. But failure was a great lesson.

Whenever I had a question, Dad was there. He gave me plenty of leeway, but I see now he was guiding the whole process. That summer I saw in action the power of advocates to help me learn and grow!

Results of Developing Key Advocates

Human beings are designed to connect and enjoy relationships in every arena of life. When the opposite happens, we feel pain. Many people know the emptiness of a home losing love and energy. I've seen the same thing happen elsewhere. Once-caring schools can dry up. Apathy can overtake a town or city. The downplaying or death of relationships happens in the workplace all the time. When a company lacks advocates, the atmosphere suffers, employees find themselves stifled, and customers can sense a lack of caring in how they are treated. Employees end up working for a paycheck rather than passion. Days get long, and even the best workers can waste away, waiting for the clock to hit quitting time.

A healthy culture—a life-giving atmosphere—is the direct result of developing advocates, quality relationships with people who truly care for us. And those relationships deepen when we have conversations focused on real needs and a readiness to help. In fact, if you want to cultivate a great culture in any setting, the Power of 3 will help you take things to the next level.

Cultures rise and fall on relationships. And relationships depend on the quality of conversations. Talking together, with kindness and honesty, one-on-one and in groups, is how *everything* positive happens that will affect the health of a culture. Here's a simple equation you can remember:

Advocates + Caring Conversations = Healthy Culture

Advocates can come into our lives in a variety of seasons and situations. We can find them among our family, neighbors, faith community, and coworkers. Look around. Who are your best advocates today? How are you investing time with those uplifting people? What can you do to further develop those relationships? How are you widening your circle?

If you're busy and barely making it through the day, you might be saying to yourself, *I'm too busy to connect with others. I just need downtime.*

But if you see the benefit of inviting advocates into your life and want to make those relationships a priority, there are a couple of quick ways to jump-start that goal.

Your first step? Think of a handful of people you already know but have missed connecting with. Whoever comes to mind, send them a short encouraging text and ask them to grab a cup of coffee or schedule a time for a phone call. You'll be surprised at the positive lift you get just by setting up a meeting. The uplift is even greater when you get together to reacquaint yourself with an old friend or a coworker.

Your next step? Make a regular habit of *developing* advocates and *being* an advocate by setting aside just minutes each week for a few simple tasks. This small investment of time benefits everyone . . . including you! It leads to meaningful discoveries and better relationships. As you learn about others, you will grow too. You can try this in a work setting, a place with great opportunities to make a difference. Why? Because developing advocates and being an advocate for coworkers is a top area of focus if you want to be successful. As we have all heard before, we need to *be* friends to have friends. Here are three simple ways to become an advocate to others with no strings attached:

1. *Ask your teammate, boss, or coworker if there is anything you can do for them today.* Offering help makes others feel seen and valued. I'm sure you can remember an instance when you needed help and wished someone had reached out to you.

2. *Be genuine as you encourage.* Say something like, "I loved your thoughts at our meeting the other day. Very insightful." Or "I liked or enjoyed . . . (pick something)." It's amazing how little appreciation and recognition most people get at work, and it's often not difficult to find something you genuinely appreciate in another person's work.

3. *Invite a coworker for coffee, lunch, or a short walk during your break.* Try adding a new person to your circle of friends. What needs do you see around you? Who needs a listening ear? Who could use a simple opportunity to connect? If you give without expecting anything in return, you'll find everyone ends up inspired. It's a two-way street. Friends tend to become advocates.

If you're already practicing these habits at work, how about doing the same with your spouse and kids at home? Or with good friends? Or with neighbors you don't know well? Expanding your circle of advocates—and being an advocate for them—will help you all to grow.

How Advocates Increase Your Emotional Intelligence

Want to really accelerate your growth? Advocates shine when life brings adversity your way. When you see your obstacles as opportunities to go deeper with people—asking for help when you need it and giving help when you can—you strengthen the triangle. It is like driving over a bridge that is made up of many triangles equally sharing the load of the car or truck. This allows you to safely reach your destination.

Life's rough patches on the road often make us reflective. How often have you heard someone lament that they wish they had listened to past advice or gone with their gut instinct in making a decision? When you use the Power of 3 by being an advocate or inviting advocates into your life, you discover how this helps you gain clarity of mind and make more thoughtful emotional responses instead of over- or wrongly reacting. The result is that you will be far more likely to make better decisions about what the next best step is.

Suppose you and your boss are at odds, or you feel threatened that your job may be downsized. It pains you. You worry and fret. You may lose sleep. Here's a crucial point: your response to conflict, adversity, or other challenges is rooted in your emotional intelligence.

Dr. Daniel Goleman, an author and science journalist, explored how five key areas of emotional intelligence are just as important to your success and happiness as your raw intellect—how smart you are. He first wrote about his groundbreaking research in his bestselling book *Emotional Intelligence*. He points out five key areas of emotional intelligence that can be measured accurately:

- *Self-awareness*—the ability to recognize and understand your moods, emotions, and drives, as well as their effect on others
- *Self-regulation*—the ability to control or redirect disruptive impulses and moods and

the propensity to suspend judgment and think before acting

- *Personal motivation*—passion and energy to work for your own internal reasons, feeling like you're doing what you're supposed to be doing
- *Social awareness*—the ability to understand the emotional makeup of other people and how your words and actions affect them
- *Social regulation*—the ability to influence the emotional clarity of others through managing relationships and building networks[1]

Struggling in any of these five areas can impact your everyday living. It's like a five-legged stool. If legs are loose or of different lengths, we wobble. Remove legs altogether, and we fall off. We end up compensating for the unbalanced stool, and we'll likely think, say, or do things that aren't in anyone's best interest, whether our own or that of loved ones, colleagues, or strangers.

Here's where advocates are key. Having someone on our side who can provide context and honest feedback to us is like opening a gift. We often see our behavior from one angle, as if we're just looking at the wrapping paper on a present. But as the wrapping comes off, we get another perspective on what's really in the box—a perspective we're not likely to get on our own. Whether you need affirmation of what you're doing right or a challenge to approach a situation differently, advocates help you deepen all five domains of emotional intelligence.

I love having advocates in my life. With time and effort, I've cultivated wonderful advocates who help when business and personal challenges arise. I count on friends who care for me just as I am, with all my frailty. Equally important are the close spiritual advocates I can talk to any time of the day or night.

Marshal Your Advocates to Win

Again, I ask the question: Where could you use help today? Who can come alongside you to help you grow as a person or develop in ways that advance your career? Whether you place a high or low value on relationships, your connections with others grow stronger only if you consciously commit to cultivating them and taking them to deeper levels.

**One of the paradoxes of modern society
is that we can be surrounded by people,
have a long list of contacts in our phones,
and register many friends on our Facebook
pages or LinkedIn profiles, yet feel intensely
alone–and lack true advocates.**

The list of reasons we may be cut off from possible advocates is as long as a Minnesota winter, but it can include pride; shyness; mistrust of others; insecurity; busyness; unrealistic expectations; an unwillingness to share on a deep level; and a tendency to push others away by being too needy, talkative, or dominant. Given the many potential obstacles to successful relationships, it's a wonder we have anyone to talk to at all!

John Cacioppo, a leading psychologist specializing in the study of loneliness, reported that loneliness not only speeds up death in sick people but also makes healthy people sick by putting them into a stressful fight-or-flight mode. Statistics tell us that men are lonelier than women, and the retired are lonelier than the employed.[2]

An AARP loneliness study surveyed 3,012 Americans age 45 and older. It found that:

- 35 percent of adults 45 and up are lonely.
- Over 42.6 million older adult Americans suffer from chronic loneliness.
- Those in poor health are more likely to be lonely.[3]

These are ominous facts and figures. It's possible, however, to make those necessary connections.

Transformational Coaching

Christine is a living example of how inviting advocates makes all the difference. She was a director at a major manufacturing company. Her aggressiveness came across as a lack of respect and trust for the people working under her. Her manner made it impossible to create strong working relationships with her team members and peers. Everyone's performance (not to mention feelings) suffered. Christine's boss asked me to work with her.

To assist Christine, I relied on each point of the Power of 3. First, I asked her the right questions: "What is your end goal? What do you really want? What is your motivation for wanting that?" I learned that Christine wanted a few things: to be a great leader in order to help the company grow, to be a better communicator, and to have better relationships with her staff.

The next step was to identify Christine's God-given gifts and see whether she was fully utilizing them. To do that, we assembled a five-member team of advocates from among her staff and asked them a series of questions about Christine that explored her communication, leadership, empathy, listening, analytical, and motivational skills. The results showed Christine where her strengths were, where she was excelling, and where she needed to improve.

Finally, we created a plan for Christine that clearly defined goals for making changes in her leadership and communication style and how we would measure her progress. Once again, advocates played a key role. Over the next four months, her advocate team provided weekly feedback on how Christine was doing. In addition, I met with Christine biweekly to go over her team's responses and review her growth.

The outcome was remarkable. Christine rediscovered her talents, moved away from her fears, made huge strides as a leader and communicator, and developed much warmer relationships with her staff, who became consistent advocates.

I called Christine's road map to growth a "Foundation of Excellence" plan. You can create your own plan, enlist advocates to help you overcome your obstacles, and grow into the person you are meant to be. As with Christine, you can draw on each point in the Power of 3 triangle.

Coaching with the GAME System

I find that a system is most effective when we need consistency to make lasting progress toward something of value. I introduced the GAME system years ago in my practice because I have personally found systems so rewarding in my own life. One small example of a system I use is when to change the blades on my razor and the brush head on my toothbrush. I used to keep using the same blades until I cut my face, because I would just forget when to replace them. Then I read the importance of putting a new brush head on my automatic toothbrush. I came up with a simple system to know when to change both items. I now change both blades and brush on the first and the fifteenth of each month, and I don't have to think about it anymore: it has become second nature. I also don't cut my face anymore! That's the beauty of having a system.

Your GAME steps to create a system for your growth might start with

G—Get a *goal* that is important to you. Set one and write it down!

A—*Ask* advocates into your world who are willing to be supportive.

M—*Measure* how you will know when you are making progress on a short-term basis.

E—*Evaluate* the end result by what you are learning and the kind of person you are becoming in the process of achieving your goal.

So where might you begin?

- Invite a specific advocate to collaborate with you, someone you trust who can serve as a friend, mentor, and accountability partner. What if you can't think of anyone? Ask someone in the area of your interest for a person's name and call them to meet for a cup of coffee. Many times your church, clubs like Rotary, or business leaders will know someone who could be an advocate if you give them specifics about what you are looking for and why. You may just need a person to bounce a few ideas off, or if it is something more profound, like making a Foundations of Excellence plan, you might benefit from getting a coach.

- Together with your accountability partner, ask the same important questions I asked Christine—begin with the GAME system.

> **GOAL:** Set your end goal. What do you really want? What is your motivation for wanting that?
>
> **ASK:** Ask your team of trustworthy advocates (even if it is just one person) to speak truthfully and with your best interests in mind. I always send them a few simple survey questions to answer. These are designed to pinpoint your talents and other relevant questions that can help move you toward your goals. Try using the "Uplifting Circle" activity in chapter 5 (see pages 104–106).

MEASURE: Share how you plan to measure your progress.

EVALUATE: Finally, as you open up and share your goals, ask those same advocates to partner with you over the next two to four months. Evaluating is simply reflecting on the feedback you receive and your own feelings about how you are doing. Ultimately, it is what we learn and what we become through our journey that brings transformation. I know this will accelerate your progress, and you most likely will develop lifelong friendships in the process.

When you apply the Power of 3 in this manner, you'll discover perspectives and opportunities you never imagined.

If time is limited or your advocates don't live nearby, a short e-mail, video chat, or phone call is all it takes to get the information and encouragement you need to move forward!

Facing Adversity—Family, Friends, and Faith

Perhaps the hardest time to reach out for advocates is when you experience dire need. Those times call for naked honesty—maybe more honesty than you've ever shown about the hurts you're tempted to hide from others.

I was in that situation as my cancer treatments went on and on. I knew I was surrounded by people who cared about what I was going through. They were advocates by sending e-mails and notes and by checking in with calls and texts. But I was at a desperate point where I especially needed their help. So I sent out an e-mail to my most treasured allies.

To put this letter into context, all my hair was falling out. Rather than looking goofy, I went to my barber and asked her to at least clean up what little hair was left. Here is the e-mail I sent:

Dear friends,
I walked out of the strip mall today, and for the
first time in my life, the wind no longer bothered
my hair. You know how it is . . . the wind whips
its way across your head, and you constantly
take your hand to try and brush your hair back
in place. Well, I no longer have that problem
since all my hair is now gone. This is one of the
advantages to having had aggressive chemo from
Mayo. It is so strong and toxic that you get to
do a makeover when the chemo ends, and you
get a whole new set of hair! Another advantage
is I have no need for Jenny Craig, Nutrisystem,
Weight Watchers, or any program of that nature.
I have lost twenty pounds and have the dubious
distinction of being at my college freshman
weight!

I have attached a photo celebrating my new
look, knowing that I am going to be healed and
that the Lord is using medicine as the avenue.

Personally, I wish God would just heal me and I wouldn't have to go through this tough time, but I trust in the ultimate victory. The other picture of Pam and myself is down at the Reynolds Plantation, where Pam's sister Nan and her husband, Greg, have a beautiful home, and we visited just before beginning this journey. This was the last picture where I had hair.

Last week I spent five days in the hospital but made it through, and this week has been great. We return to Mayo this coming Tuesday for the

*second of six rounds of chemo. Each session lasts
all day, and I think when I leave, there must be
a "glow" about me from all these toxins! This
has been the hardest thing I have ever had to do.
Thankfully, I have a wonderful wife who has
been so helpful, supportive, and encouraging.*

*So if you can pray this week, I just want this
to work and to kill off the awful cancer and
the many tumors in my body. Also, we need his
grace going through everything because it is just
plain hard. Many tears have been shed, and
I appreciate the small things in life like never
before.*

*But I am an optimist and we will "win" with
the Lord's help. Have a wonderful weekend.*

Robb

I sent this e-mail to about a hundred people who
I knew had a genuine interest in how my treatments
were going. I received an incredible outpouring of
love, encouragement, and specific prayers in reply.
Nearly everyone mentioned how inspiring they
thought the message was because of my hope in God.

Nearly everyone mentioned how this short update lifted their spirits and nudged them to think about their own need for faith.

I didn't write the note to be inspiring. Honestly, I felt tired. At times, I felt numb and empty. I did, however, want to express how my faith in God was helping me and that through the worst of times, we can all find the positive if we just look up.

> **With fighting for my life a daily thought, I began to focus on what I could do versus what I couldn't do.**

Monitoring the state of my immune system was constant. If my blood work was okay on a Monday, I could go out with a handful of people and eat at a small restaurant. If my blood counts were low, I was relegated to wearing a mask and locking myself up at home even on the loveliest summer day. If I caught a bug, the doctors might not be able to stop the infection. I would most likely die.

So I focused on writing notes and calling people to encourage them. I talked on the phone with my clients to offer insight where I could. I listened to uplifting talks, sermons, and inspiring messages by people with something positive to share.

I'm not sure I would have made it through this journey without my faith in God. The most amazing changes were simple ones, and they still go on today. I began to thank God for each day, and I really meant it. I relished every walk, every short boat ride with Bentley on my lap, and every moment of holding Pam's hand.

In many ways, through facing death I became more alive because I noticed the good that life brought me every day.

And now? I still wake up and thank God for each day. Every day is truly a "great day." The battle with three cancers and all the aftereffects of the treatments have allowed me to see what I often missed in the busyness of life before my illness. My faith gave me hope and strength through the five months of being so sick. As my friend Jon would say in his humorous way when I was lying on the couch, "Robb, it is far better to be seen than viewed!"

Transform Their World—and Yours

As you can see from my story above, inviting advocates isn't simply about getting help. It's just as much about giving aid wherever you can. I sent an e-mail to enlist the support of my advocates, and they were uplifted in the process.

But we should also be intentional about being advocates for others. Studies show that committing conscious acts of kindness leads to better mental health for both the giver and the receiver. And like a pebble dropped in a pond that sends ripples in every direction, the impact of a single caring act can spread far beyond the moment. When we advocate for others, we set love in motion that spreads around the world. Love works!

Christine, the manufacturing company director, found these reciprocal properties of advocacy to be true. When she changed her communication style by soliciting the opinions of her team and becoming a better listener, she turned into their advocate—which allowed her colleagues to explore and lean into their own talents without fear of being ignored or chastised by their director.

By helping executives and their team members develop their talents and improve their communication and leadership skills, I've watched thousands of people grow into their purpose both professionally and personally. In turn, serving as an advocate for them has blessed me. I've enjoyed the deep satisfaction that comes from living out my own calling and have made many lifelong friends.

The same has been true in my personal life. When a colleague and friend, Bob Benedict, was struggling with his business, I began meeting with him in the mornings to listen and offer encouragement and insights from my own experience. He did the same for me. This went on for years. I believe those meetings played at least a small part in the success of Bob's new career, and the same was true for my growth. Isn't that how it goes? When we encourage or advise a friend, what's reflected back is often even greater than the light we put out.

Today, Bob is a nationally recognized negotiation expert—and as one of my best friends, he is also one of my most-valued advocates. I could also say the same of my friend Jon Barnett. I met Jon and his wife, Mary Jo, when I was 2,500 miles away from Minnesota at a Sunday-morning church service. Midway through the service, the pastor asked us to turn around and greet someone we didn't know. Well, that wasn't too tough for me as I'd never been there before! As I turned around, Jon extended his hand to shake mine and asked where we were from. I shared that Minneapolis was my home, but we were now living in Irvine, California. He said, "No way! We're from Minnesota as well!" Jon and I became best friends, and thirty years later we see each other often and are mutual advocates for each other. It started with me putting my hand out to Jon, and I've been blessed by that returned handshake.

> **Put simply, the best way to invite advocates into your life is to become one. Use the Power of 3 to get you there. When people see that you genuinely care about their welfare and want to support them, they will naturally reciprocate.**

Tracy Warshal was at a Georgia grocery store when she noticed that a man in the checkout line ahead of her had forgotten his wallet. She made an instant decision to be his advocate and pay for his few items. The man thanked Tracy, but later he did much more than that. When the man learned that Tracy worked at Piedmont Cancer Institute, he donated ten thousand dollars to the Piedmont Foundation, which funds new equipment, research, and education programs for health care in the Atlanta area. Though she hadn't planned it or expected it, Tracy stepping up with a small gesture encouraged a stranger to become an advocate for better health care that would impact many lives.

The key is your motivation. People will quickly sense self-interest or an attempt to manipulate them and will turn away. Love, on the other hand, always attracts! Who needs a call or text from you today?

Practicing the Power of 3

Hopefully after reading this chapter, you know how you can invite advocates into your life and become one to others. Here are a few more questions to get you thinking about inviting and becoming an advocate.

1. How would you describe the culture of the department you work in, the overall company, or your culture at home on a scale of 1 to 10 (10 is outstanding)?

2. Culture rises and falls on relationships. What can you do using the Power of 3 to improve the culture in your sphere of influence?

3. Bridges, floor trusses, and roof trusses are all triangles because their strength comes from three equal sides working together. What additions in the advocate triangle of family, friends, and faith would most help you become a better person or leader?

4. Despite the many "friends" we have across social media platforms like Facebook and LinkedIn, people of all ages are experiencing loneliness. What might you do to be more of an advocate to others?

5. Transformational coaching and leading occurs more frequently when we are advocates. How can the GAME system help you and others that you care for?

ASK

THE
POWER
OF 3

ADVOCATE   ACTIVATE

PART 4

Living in the Triangle

CHAPTER 8

Coaching Yourself and Others in the Power of 3: Small Beginnings—Big Results

The only thing worse than training your employees and having them leave is not training them and having them stay.

HENRY FORD

THE LAST THING I WAS THINKING when I got the diagnosis of three cancers was, *Oh boy, this is a prime opportunity for me to develop endurance and strength!* No. I gulped, took a deep breath, and fumbled for a response. I'm seldom at a loss for words, and the tough circumstances I'd already survived through the years had given me the ability to succeed when hit with devastating news. But this was a lot to take in.

Few things in life are 100 percent predictable. Sure, death and taxes. But there's another part of life we all have in common and all end up facing, with some degree of failure or success. We all suffer setbacks with family members, difficult people at work, the loss of friendships, or the disappointment that our best plans just haven't turned out the way we thought they would. *Why didn't I get that promotion? Why didn't I see that annoying habit of my spouse when we were dating? Why isn't this working out?*

Adversity is like a car accident. You certainly don't want it. You think you can dodge it. But it happens anyway. The accident might come as a glancing blow. Or as a full broadside hit. Or, sometimes, as a head-on collision.

Everyone faces adversity, whether we call it "drama" or "troubles" or a "dark night of the soul." The Power of 3 allows us to keep walking and discover better paths.

An ancient writer talked about adversity and obstacles as a predictable part of life. He wrote, "We are pressed on every side by troubles, but we are not crushed. We are perplexed, but not driven to despair. We are hunted down, but never abandoned by God.

We get knocked down, but we are not destroyed" and "trials . . . help us develop endurance."[1] I haven't always enthusiastically shared his perspective.

Years ago, I was running a high-tech company when I learned that four individuals I thought were loyal employees left, all at once. They decided to start a company that would compete directly with mine.

I wish I'd developed the Power of 3 way back then, as I desperately could have used a different approach. I made so many mistakes in how I responded. Anger and retaliation ate away at me and caused many sleepless nights. The turmoil dragged on, and I felt it impacting my appetite, general attitude, and ability to deal with even small daily challenges. I'd get so angry when I was cut off on a Los Angeles freeway or I was delayed at the store because the person in front of me was slow in paying.

The stress wasn't good for me. But all this changed when I met with Bob, a fellow businessperson. After listening to me explain the betrayal of what had happened, this highly successful leader asked me a simple question: "Robb, who is in charge?" I remember slumping back in my chair, reflecting for a moment, and saying with a sigh of relief, "God is, if I let him be."

Small Beginnings, Big Results

Something powerful was happening. My friend was modeling the first principle of becoming a great coach. In this simple exchange, the power of asking the right questions set the stage for an immediate transformation of my thinking. Whether you're coaching yourself, informally coaching others, or dealing with people in business, start here!

This simple beginning changed how I talked to myself, how I felt, and how I acted. It led me down a far better decision-making path. It was a small beginning that led to a big result.

After unsuccessfully trying to talk with the group who left the company and wrestling with the fact that they took customers with them, I decided to forgo pursuing a legal pathway. With the team that remained, I focused on doing right for our customers and doubled our efforts to serve. Within months, the business rebounded and continued to grow exponentially.

The right question Bob asked moved me from feeling like a victim to taking personal responsibility for everything. This included my emotions, empathy for others, and being the leader I needed to be at the company. Once I made that important decision, my appetite, energy, peace of mind, and clarity of thought returned.

Of course, you know this principle is the first element of the Power of 3—ask the right questions. But have you thought of yourself as a coach, the kind of helper that Bob was to me—first a coach to yourself, then to family and friends, and then to those you might lead at work? When you understand the Power of 3, you will have all it takes to make an enormous difference for yourself and for everyone within your reach.

To be a good coach, you need to be a good listener. And to be a good listener, you need to ask good questions.

The Power of 3 will elevate you in whatever role you find yourself because you'll abundantly meet two fundamental human needs—the needs to be heard and to be valued.

How to Coach Yourself with the Power of 3

The best coaches in the world know how to apply their methodology to themselves. The Power of 3 isn't simply a nice idea to read about and put on the shelf, an emergency kit to pull out when you experience a head-on collision. The Power of 3 is an everyday, moment-by-moment habit of thinking and doing. Live it!

Consider a married couple in their thirties. Brad is frustrated with his wife, Wendy. More than frustrated. Brad is angry and worried. Over the last several months, Wendy has grown increasingly distant. She's worked late multiple nights each week at her job as a web designer. She usually lets Brad know if she's going to miss dinner, though twice in the last month, she's forgotten to call. Brad knows that Wendy's company recently took on a major client and that several members of the staff are working overtime to revamp the client's marketing program. The group includes Daniel, a new copywriter. Brad realizes it might just be his imagination, but he's afraid that Wendy is having an affair.

Now it's 6:30 p.m. Brad is home from work, sitting alone at their dining room table. Wendy still isn't home. She hasn't called, and she hasn't answered either of Brad's texts. The baked salmon he prepared for their evening dinner has long since cooled. Brad, on the other hand, is steaming.

Why hasn't she called? Brad thinks. *This is Thursday—our date night. How can she be so thoughtless? Why does she always think only about herself? What is wrong with her?*

The next question that forms in Brad's mind is the one he's been trying to avoid: *Is she with Daniel?*

It takes only a minute for Brad's thoughts to build into a tidal wave. He jumps up, grabs Wendy's plate, and hurls it into the sink, sending salmon flying and shattering the china. Then he buries his face in his hands. Five minutes later, Wendy walks through the door.

Don't Get Hijacked!

Now let's imagine the same scenario with a far better outcome. Brad has just read *The Power of 3* and understands the principles of living in the triangle. That doesn't change the fact that Brad is sitting alone at his dining room table, staring at cold salmon. He's still wondering where Wendy is and why she hasn't answered his texts. He's still angry and worried. His amygdala is armed and ready. A full-throttle hijacking is already underway!

But Brad remembers what he's read. He's going to try to hijack the hijacker. Though he's tempted to run through a list of all the terrible potential reasons for why Wendy isn't home—including an affair—he decides to ask himself the right questions instead. He knows that begins with discovery.

How do I stop myself from assuming the worst? He decides to not jump to conclusions. There are many possible reasons for Wendy's absence and lack of response. She could be in a meeting that went long. Her cell phone could have died. She could have a flat tire. Brad thinks, *What could I do to find out what's actually happening?* He decides he'll wait another twenty minutes, then call Paula, Wendy's colleague at the office.

Brad isn't done with discovery questions, however.

What, he asks himself, *is really making me so concerned?* Brad realizes that with Wendy distracted and away from home more often, he's feeling insecure. Since his first wife left him for another man, Brad has sometimes struggled with fear that Wendy will do the same.

Brad shifts into proactive mode. *How can I relieve this insecure feeling? In this busy time, what can I do to help us reconnect?* It occurs to Brad that simply setting a time with Wendy to share his feelings would lift a huge weight from his shoulders. Asking the right questions leads Brad to a self-awareness that gives him more control over his emotional response.

As Brad ponders the situation, he realizes he hasn't stepped back to consider more creative solutions. *What might I do to support Wendy while she's working overtime and draw her closer?* he asks himself. *What does she need from me right now?* Brad begins to see new options. He could take over more household duties to make Wendy feel supported. If she needs to work late but has time for a dinner break, he could meet her for a quick bite at a restaurant near her office. Since he knows she dislikes refueling at the gas station, he could even take her car out and fill it up after she gets home.

Now he's getting somewhere.

In this version of our scenario, asking just a few right questions has helped Brad see new possibilities to alleviate his concerns and improve his marriage. Five minutes later, when Wendy walks through the door, he's in a better state of mind. Instead of greeting her with accusations—"Why didn't you answer my texts? Why are you so late?"—he's calm, curious about her day, open to hearing what Wendy has to say, and ready to seek positive solutions for this stressful season of overtime.

You'll find similar results as you begin proactively coaching yourself, applying the power of asking the right questions to your life. We talked about the different types of questions in chapter 3, so here's a reminder of the three different tools to help you:

Do a Self-Talk Assessment

We've seen how negative self-talk can trigger a stress response to trials, increasing the chances of an

amygdala hijacking and making it more difficult to ask the right questions. The following two-question assessment will give you a better idea of how you deal with adversity, whether relatively small (a boss you don't like or a friend who's ignoring you) or large (a grim health diagnosis or an important relationship issue). For each question, circle your score of 1 to 5.

Let's say you discover a person at work has said

some unkind words about you to others. Or you've learned you have a serious financial, medical, or relational problem that needs immediate attention. How do you react?

When I come across a difficult situation, my first reaction is usually *emotional* (frustration, anger, fear, impatience, etc.).	Circle your score: 1—Never 2—Not often 3—Sometimes 4—Frequently 5—Most of the time
When I'm confronted with the unknown or a real obstacle I didn't create, my reaction causes me to *make decisions* that in hindsight prove to be hurtful to myself and others.	Circle your score: 1—Never 2—Not often 3—Sometimes 4—Frequently 5—Most of the time

My Total Score: ___

Combine your scores.

- **If your total is 6 or higher,** growing your ability to ask yourself the right questions is probably your first step in self-coaching.
- **If your total is 4 or lower,** you're building a habit of engaging in healthy self-talk. Keep that up! As you coach yourself, pay special attention

to the activate and advocate points of the Power of 3 triangle.

When we learn to coach ourselves, we don't have to live in a state of constant stress.

By employing the first point in the Power of 3 triangle—asking ourselves the right questions—we take better control of our emotions, turn back an amygdala takeover, focus on the next step, and put ourselves in position to find solutions to whatever challenges block our way. It's a path toward reducing stress and gaining peace.

Coaching Family with the Power of 3

Now let's look at the next part of the triangle to see how you can use *activate* and *advocate* to informally coach others. You can engage your full power by activating your gifts and talents or helping with your presence and power as an advocate. And one of the most natural ways you can use the Power of 3 in informal coaching is with your family.

My mom is a great example of this. She constantly

THE POWER OF 3

activated her natural gifts. I bet she never once paused and said, "I should do this or that because it would look good to others." Mom truly loved and served everybody from a heart of joy. Her old-fashioned black phone book from the stationery store was bursting with hundreds of names, phone numbers, and addresses. She regularly riffled through its pages to find friends to call in order to check on them. It drove my dad nuts. He wasn't nearly as social and clearly didn't enjoy talking on the phone.

Dinner parties were common in our home, and Mom listened to others for hours. She lifted them up with her warm smile, an encouraging word, and a caring touch, and no one ever left our house without her asking if there was anything she could do to help them. Often Mom would just say, "I'll be praying for you." She knew intuitively that the secret to meaningful relationships involved being a great listener, and a great listener always asks great questions. Mom made the world better by constantly activating her gifts— her natural love for people, empathy, optimism, and encouragement. Her way of playing the game of life would have made Coach John Wooden proud. She always did the best she was capable of.

I was at my parents' retirement place in Florida when Mom threw one of her dinner parties. She cared nothing about status as the world defined it, meaning the mix of people was always eclectic and interesting. One night, Chuck Colson and his wife showed up. Colson was famous as the Watergate criminal turned faithful Christian and leader in prison reform. And that night, the Colsons were joined by the heiress of the Coca-Cola company.

The high profile of these people didn't change Mom's plans for the evening. As always, Mom served dinner and informally coached these friends by sharing an inspirational thought and giving each a Bible or other books to encourage them. Over the years, Mom gave away hundreds of books, and her guests were amazed at how she got her point across through these books!

It was all Mom's special form of informal coaching—asking questions of others and using her gifts of hospitality. She was a nonstop advocate and worked hard to connect people to faith. Guess who these guests would call when trouble came? Mom.

I saw this in action constantly while I was growing up, but I didn't grasp the depth of her impact until much later in life. Twenty-five years after Mom passed away due to breast cancer, I walked into a small restaurant in Detroit Lakes, Minnesota. It was called the Hotel Shoreham and was located by a beautiful Northwoods lake. As I walked in, I heard a shout from over by the window. "Robby! It's you! It's you!" I immediately recognized two ladies as Mom's old friends. They were well into their late eighties, if not older. I immediately greeted them with a big hug. Without any prompting, these old friends talked about how much they loved Mom and how they missed her laugh and smile. They sighed as they talked about her. They still really missed her—even several decades after she had passed away!

What a legacy Mom left. She knew how to ask great questions and listen intently to understand what was going on in a person's life. She activated her talents and became an advocate for so many people by saying the right thing (sometimes by saying nothing at all) and by following up with action. As an informal coach, Mom was a rock star.

My parents each had their own style of loving and connecting. Dad was also a great coach, but his way was to deliver a kick in the pants when I needed to get back on track and to ask questions like "How do you expect to . . . ?" When Dad spent time with me and talked with me while fishing or golfing, I felt loved.

Here's the thing: my parents were constantly—and naturally—coaching my siblings and me but without our realizing it. They encouraged us to connect with faith, family, and friends, and family dinners were a normal part of life, where we often benefited from their wisdom and questions.

Mom's coaching was very different from Dad's, but they were both effective in our lives. Maybe your God-given gifts don't line up with my mom's. Maybe you find yourself more reserved, and you wonder how you might coach your own family. The point isn't for your coaching to look just like Mom's or Dad's. The point is for you to recognize your God-given talents and activate them for the benefit of your family in a way that is natural for you. What would it look like for you to activate your talents in your family and to be an advocate for them? The common thread is making sure that whatever your style of coaching, it needs to be done with love. Love looks like listening and understanding. We help, support, encourage, or guide people when they feel our concern or love—not our overreacting in anger. Anger is like turning off the lights in any meaningful communication. It shuts it down and is not helpful. Asking great questions is your best tool to turn the lights back on.

But what if the family you grew up in was different from mine? Maybe there was one parent struggling to find time to parent, or you moved around a lot and friends were harder to make. What if you didn't receive the kind of coaching I received? Can you still become an informal coach to friends or acquaintances even if you lacked an ideal upbringing? The answer is absolutely yes!

Becoming a Memorable Coach as a Friend

The Power of 3 will allow you to bond more quickly with others, readily understand their situation, and help you guide them to the next step and beyond. The key skill you need is the willingness to be a good listener. I say "skill" because I know anyone can become a good listener if they want to.

Here are some ways, using the Power of 3, that you can develop your skill as a good listener:

1. Always begin at the first point of the Power of 3 triangle by asking great questions. You can use the various DIP questions as a wonderful way to listen and understand what is going on.

Really listening does something that we all need and want–to be heard and valued. Asking questions naturally helps us care for others. People inevitably feel more valued.

2. When the other person answers your questions, you'll know what natural talents you need to activate as the person opens the door for you to help. If you don't know what help you can possibly offer in a difficult situation, ask more questions. Doing so might help your friend to see the next step. At some point, just ask, "What do you think might be a next step?" It's

amazing how many times people already know the answer.

3. When a friend is struggling emotionally, use a simple scale—a numerical choice—to help that person step back and gain clarity. Ask, "On a scale of 1 to 10, what impact is this having on your stress level or on your being at peace?" (1 means little impact, and 10 means completely overwhelmed).

This question taps into the other person's prefrontal cortex and helps restore order amid chaos. In extreme emotional situations, it elicits logic. The key is to help your friend rate how he or she feels or thinks about the specific issue at hand—not the whole of life, but the need of the moment. Once your friend assigns a number, you can begin to break down what the number really means and let your friend just talk it out. This approach defuses drama, reaffirms your friendship, and communicates that you understand and value your friend.

4. Sometimes it becomes obvious how you can be an advocate for the person, often through more

questions. This might take the form of asking whether the person is connected to family or other friends or where your friend is with regard to faith. An example might be as simple as asking, "Who might be helpful to you in taking the next step?" or "How might your circle of friends or faith community be of support?" or "What can I do to help?"

Being a good listener is a great way to coach your friends, and living in the triangle of the Power of 3 will give you the tools you need to naturally and effectively coach those closest to you.

How to Be a Rock Star Coach at Work

With the Power of 3, you can make an indelible mark at work by starting the same way with team members or employees as you would with coaching yourself and being an informal coach with friends or family.

The rock star leaders I've coached over the years have discovered the power of leading with the heart. It's their secret to getting remarkable results.

When I was coaching a wonderful leader, Heather, our conversation eventually turned to how she could best motivate a certain team member. By now, I hope you know where I started—asking questions! I asked Heather the right questions, and I activated my gifts of discernment and understanding to uncover what was really happening with the employee. Heather then considered what talents she could bring to the situation. After listening intently, I asked her what her best next step might be, and we talked through many ideas. She began the conversation bubbling with frustration. By the end, she came to her own conclusion of what needed to happen and wrote out an action plan.

Your best opportunities for using the Power of 3 at work often depend on your structure and level of authority. Consider this:

- Anyone can use the Power of 3 to lead by *example*. How you live in the Power of 3 will speak volumes to others. Let them wonder about—and ask—what motivates you to stay focused on what really matters, steadfastly

maximize your own gifts, and bring out the
best in others. Then you can share the simple
truth of the Power of 3.

- Anyone can use the Power of 3 to lead by
  influence. You likely spend much of your
  workday in teams or matrix organizations
  where you have little real control over others.
  You can go about your job using the Power
  of 3 to make a standout contribution to your
  team and persuade others to pull their weight—
  not just telling them to do their work but
  helping them to excel.

- Many situations invite you to lead by *instruction*.
  You might interact with leaders far above
  you in the organizational chart. When you
  have occasions for discussion, be known for
  asking the right questions. Know how you
  can activate your gifts for the good of the
  company. And become an advocate for those
  who need help spotlighting their own talents.
  Say, "So-and-so would be great at that. Let
  me explain."

- If you are in a formal leadership role, you can also lead by *accountability*. As you lead people on your team—those who report to you—all kinds of levers of power are available to you. Many target *external motivation*, like the carrot of bestowing titles and offering pay increases or bonuses. Or like the stick of threatening someone's status or job. The Power of 3 is your opportunity to leverage *internal* or *intrinsic motivation*. One of the first keys in leading or coaching is to understand what is really motivating a person. We use a scientific instrument to do so in my practice, but you can also just ask a person why they do what they do. It may take a few follow-up questions and your own observations to find out. But it is worth it! The boss who uses the Power of 3 helps people work hard because they want to—not simply because they have to.

When you use the Power of 3, people will experience you as the solid truss of a floor, or the strong roof overhead, or the triangle of a bridge that supports the weight of whatever comes its way.

Implementing the Power of 3 on the job makes you a trusted ally like no other. Don't be surprised when people up, down, and across the organization say, "I love working with you!"

It really doesn't make any difference whether you're coaching yourself, informally coaching family or friends, or being a rock star coach at work. The method and outcomes are all the same.

Small beginnings. Big results. Wow!

Practicing the Power of 3

The Power of 3 will help you to be an effective coach for others in your life. But before you can be of the most help to others, you need to coach yourself. Answer these questions and consider the steps you might take in the next challenge you face:

1. What is the most recent stressful situation you've faced? What did that situation do to your emotions?

2. How did you respond? How did you feel about your response?

3. Write down some of the right questions you might have asked yourself at the beginning of your stressful situation. How would asking these questions have changed the result for the better?

4. What steps can you take to prepare for the next stressful situation you will face?

CONCLUSION

The Joy of Living in the Triangle: Help Yourself and Others Live Again

I am so optimistic, I'd go after Moby Dick in a rowboat and take the tartar sauce with me.

ZIG ZIGLAR

THERE'S SOMETHING AMAZING about weddings, when two people vow their lifelong love to each other and experience a new beginning. It's a beautiful moment for the couple, with family and friends gathered around, all hoping for nothing but the best ahead. And weddings inspire those of us looking on to revisit our own passion and commitment.

For me, staying alive long enough to attend one particular wedding—the marriage ceremony of my son, Ryan, and his beautiful bride-to-be, Amber—was a goal that helped me through painful months of cancer treatments. I thought, *If I could make it until then, it would be so wonderful. And it would mean I was alive.* It wasn't as if I'd feel great about dying the moment after they said, "I do," but if that was all the life I would have the privilege of enjoying, I would accept those days with gratitude and joyfully go home to be with my Lord.

Fast-forward through those tough months of treatment to the wedding day. On a crisp day in late September, there I was. Pam was next to me, and I sat as close as I could to her, arms locked together, not caring about rumpling my suit or her beautiful dress. I watched as Bentley loped down the aisle, the wedding rings attached to his collar. I listened to the pastor's words of encouragement to Ryan and Amber. And I saw the bride and groom speak their vows before God. I was so happy to see them together. I teared up, overwhelmed.

I was glad to be upright and breathing through the spring of my diagnosis and all through the summer. Even so, there was never a guarantee I'd be present that day. I'd had a PET scan in early summer, midway through my treatments, that gave us reason to hope the cancer was retreating. But I continued several more noxious rounds of chemotherapy, each worse than the last.

Finally, on the Monday before the wedding, Pam and I took another trip to Mayo for blood work and a PET scan, one last screening at the end of my chemotherapy. With the wedding less than a week away, the big picture of finishing treatments was almost lost in thoughts of the celebration. We were excited about that day, and for a moment the preparations gave us something to think about besides my looming health issues. Whatever we heard that day—good or bad—we would press on, knowing we would get through whatever followed. But being at the wedding came down to this: if my results were good, I could attend. If not, I'd be forced to stay home, far from the crowd with their swarming germs. In that case, my protests wouldn't matter. My wife, my kids, and my doctor wouldn't let me risk infection and put my life on the line, no matter how special the day.

At 5:45 a.m. on checkup day, I had a PET scan, then a blood draw. At 11 a.m., Pam and I walked into my hematologist's office. The doctor was grinning. That's a big deal. Now, to put this in perspective, most cancer doctors aren't especially upbeat. They're the people who hold steady when a patient's world shakes like an earthquake. Oncologists are measured, analytical, and diplomatic. So I was surprised to see my doctor smiling!

He put up a picture of my original PET scan from five months earlier, lit up red with all the cancer in my stomach, abdomen, and throat. Then he put up the picture taken early that morning—not a red spot anywhere in my body. It was the confirmation we dreamed of. He announced, "I have the best news I can give you. You have no cancer."

Pam and I gawked at the side-by-side photos, rejoicing with a happiness that is hard to put into words. Two things were clear to us. First, I'd be at the wedding. Second, I was more than alive. I was *healed*.

Being around a crowd of people for the wedding was just the start. Three cancers were gone. It was a final all-clear notice. We thanked God and left that day in awe of a miracle.

Celebration

I arrived home in a daze. One evening that week, a wonderful neighbor, Jeff, came over and took me out for dinner at Hazeltine National Golf Club (home of the 2016 Ryder Cup). I was in heaven. After eating a delicious meal, Jeff apologized that he had to get home but wanted my opinion on something he was doing in the backyard. As we turned the back corner of his house, a crowd of neighbors who had secretly gathered started cheering and clapping at the astonishing news of my being healed.

Jeff and his wife, Erin, had invited them, and I was stunned. Speechless. I'd never had a party like this. There was a large cake of celebration, and all the neighborhood kids had made an enormous banner and signed their names on it. I won't forget that day!

Our neighbors were doing once again what they had done all along: being true advocates for Pam and me along this journey. They had helped by mowing our lawn and stopping by to encourage us during the months of treatment. The Beckering family even gave me a T-shirt emblazoned with this quote on the back: "**Heal Can**cer:

With God Nothing Will Be Impossible—Luke 1:37."
And now we were all celebrating. Together.

Living Again

After the wedding, I had to readjust to normal life. I'd dropped to only 140 pounds, and a strong wind could move me. I needed to gain weight and strength. I began to feel free again without worrying what the next blood test would reveal. I discovered the freedom of not having to stay away from people for fear of infection. I could now be with a group of friends instead of just one at a time. The mindset shift took at least six months before I felt things were normal.

One of the first things I did was run over to the golf course and hit some balls. I was so weak that after a dozen swings, I had to sit down and rest. A flight of stairs would leave me gasping. But believe it or not, I couldn't wait to mow the grass again. Although I could do only a small square before wearing out, I smiled the whole time I walked behind the mower, gleeful like a toddler with a push toy.

I was happy before cancer. Post-cancer, you might conclude I'm delirious.

Wiggling my toes in grass was a victory. Walking in a crowd was a victory. Waking up each day knowing I was going to live was comforting and motivating. I still had to stay out of the sun most of the time and wear a hat to cover my bald head. Minor inconveniences.

A few months later, I was asked to speak for the business organization that originated the tools I use to assess leaders for hiring and promotion. Every year, the TTI Success Insights Conference dinner in Phoenix, Arizona, concludes with passing out awards to top consultants across the globe, a cadre of about three thousand. The most prestigious award is named after the company's founder, Bill Bonnstetter, and is given to the consultant who best represents the firm and the profession of consulting.

I was a little giddy just being at the conference and watching all the awards given out to others. When the emcee announced the winner of the Bill Bonnstetter Lifetime Achievement Award, I heard my name. Pam was awash with tears as the host asked me to step up to the podium. Standing at the microphone, I was dumbfounded, but as I returned to my seat, I looked up and said, "Thank you, God. Wow!"

THE POWER OF 3

After everything we had endured that year, this was an incredible honor. The award cemented in me the desire and obligation to do something more with my second chance at living.

My Journey Today

The journey continues. There are the normal struggles. Adversity never leaves us, and it can walk through our door at any time. However, I know the difference in dealing with the inevitable trials and challenges with the Power of 3, an approach born in business that was instrumental in helping me make it through the toughest time of my life. Most important, my students and clients over the years have experienced similar success in their areas of need. And this can be the same for you!

I no longer need to return to the doctor every three months for a PET scan and blood work. I recently had my two-year checkup, and again my hematologist was unusually upbeat. As he put my latest PET scan up on the big screen, he said, "Robb, your scan is perfect. You no longer have any cancer. Everything is normal."

And then my doctor said, "I don't know if you believe in God, but . . ." Pam interrupted his sentence—"We sure do!" The doctor just smiled. He had made his point as he sent us on our way.

I am living differently today, with a renewed zest for life and thankfulness for each day. I am learning to live again. I get a wonderful opportunity to become a better person—a better listener, a better husband, and a better father. When I stumble, I just look up and remember the power of the triangle as I learn to ask, activate, and advocate with the gift of family, friends, and my faith.

So what about you? What are you facing today? What is your best next step? And how might you help a friend or coworker?

The Power of 3 can improve anyone's life. It can help you lead effectively, build trust, be a rock star coach, and overcome adversity so you can live with joy. Living in the triangle will give you strength daily.

So as we end our time together and you begin to live in the Power of 3 triangle, I have three prayers for you:

May you learn to better lead with the heart by asking the right, life-giving questions.

May you discover and activate more of your gifts and talents, thriving as you do what comes naturally.

And as you become an advocate for your friends and family and live out your faith, may you develop deeper relationships fundamental to living a life where the final words you hear will be "Well done, my good and faithful servant."

A Note from Robb

THANK YOU FOR INVESTING in yourself by reading *The Power of 3*. I want you to grow, so I invite you to go to my website www.robbhiller.com. There you can get free downloads and helpful tools. If you want to go deeper, you can enroll in a digital course to use for yourself or to help develop your team. Last, I'd love to hear from you. My e-mail address is robb@performancesolutionsmn.com. Regardless of what you encounter today, each part of the triangle is there to inspire and help you.

Acknowledgments

To my wife, Pam: Thank you for caring for me through the many doctor visits and treatments. You were my rock, supporter, and encourager during these tough times. I love you. You are amazing!

To my support team at Tyndale, a great team of consummate professionals who helped bring the message of the Power of 3 into a book: All of you are such a delight to work with. Thank you!

To my medical caregivers: Thank you, Fairview Southdale Hospital doctors and nurses. You are an amazing group of caring people who truly put me first and made a huge difference in my recovery. Fairview worked together with Mayo Clinic when I qualified for a trial drug, and I lift a toast to both and say thank you! Thank you to all the nurses and doctors for your expertise, which helped me survive and eventually thrive.

To family, friends, and business encouragers: A big hug to all of you for your prayers, calls, and practical deeds of kindness. I also thank Michael Palgon and Jim Lund for their ideas for the book, their outline, and their expertise.

To my writer, Kevin Johnson: Thank you for helping me through those areas of the book where I needed your inspiration and clarity. Your experience in authoring seventy books and helping countless other writers was so calming and brought needed wisdom to this message. Thank you for your coaching, expertise, and friendship.

Notes

CHAPTER 2: CHANGE YOUR PERSPECTIVE

1. I should note that *why* questions can be helpful in a creative brainstorming session where the goal is to come up with options. However, in most everyday circumstances, *why* takes us down paths that lead to a dead end.
2. Stuart Firestein, *Ignorance: How It Drives Science* (New York: Oxford University Press, 2012), 11.

CHAPTER 3: DIP INTO YOUR TOOLBOX

1. Warren Berger, *A More Beautiful Question: The Power of Inquiry to Spark Breakthrough Ideas* (New York: Bloomsbury USA, 2014), 206.
2. Berger, 208.
3. Warren Berger, *The Book of Beautiful Questions: The Powerful Questions That Will Help You Decide, Create, Connect, and Lead* (New York: Bloomsbury USA, 2018).

CHAPTER 5: PLUG INTO YOUR GIFTS

1. Amy Adkins, "What Millennials Want from Work and Life," Gallup, May 10, 2016, https://www.gallup.com/workplace/236477/millennials-work-life.aspx .

CHAPTER 6: INVITE ADVOCATES INTO YOUR LIFE

1. Ben Sasse, *Them: Why We Hate Each Other—and How to Heal,* (New York: St. Martin's Press, 2018), 3.
2. John 13:34
3. John 15:13
4. Galatians 6:2

5. Galatians 6:5

6. Bryan Walsh, "Does Spirituality Make You Happy?" *Time*, August 7, 2017, https://time.com/4856978/spirituality-religion-happiness/.

7. Melanie Curtin, "Neuroscience Reveals 50-Year-Olds Can Have the Brains of 25-Year-Olds If They Do This 1 Thing," *Inc.*, October 23, 2018, https://www.inc.com/melanie-curtin/neuroscience-shows -that-50-year-olds-can-have-brains-of-25-year-olds-if-they-do-this .html.

8. Sue McGreevey, "Eight Weeks to a Better Brain," *Harvard Gazette*, January 21, 2011, https://news.harvard.edu/gazette/story/2011/01 /eight-weeks-to-a-better-brain/.

CHAPTER 7: CULTIVATE LIFE-GIVING CONNECTIONS

1. Daniel Goleman, *Emotional Intelligence: Why It Can Matter More Than IQ* (New York: Bantam, 1995), 43–44.

2. Ben Sasse, *Them: Why We Hate Each Other—and How to Heal* (New York: St. Martin's Press, 2018), 23–24.

3. AARP, *Loneliness and Social Connections: A National Survey of Adults 45 and Older*, 2018, https://www.aarp.org/content/dam /aarp/research/surveys_statistics/life-leisure/2018/loneliness-social -connections-2018.doi.10.26419-2Fres.00246.001.pdf.

CHAPTER 8: COACHING YOURSELF AND OTHERS IN THE POWER OF 3

1. 2 Corinthians 4:8-9, NLT; Romans 5:3, NLT

About the Author

Robb Hiller is the CEO of Performance SolutionsMN. He is nationally known for his expertise in talent selection, executive coaching, team development, sales, and leadership building. He was the CEO of a high-tech company, Minnesota Business Systems, where he developed a passion for acquiring talent and solving problems executives face. After selling the company, Robb started consulting with hundreds of high-tech and medical device companies, including several Fortune 1000 companies. He was recently awarded the Bill J. Bonnstetter Lifetime Achievement Award for his extensive work in evaluating talent. He has assessed more than 24,000 people in the past twenty-five years. He is a business graduate of St. Olaf College. Robb and his wife have three adult children and live in Minnesota.